DUH-VOTIONS

Other Books by Sue Buchanan

I'm Alive and the Doctor's Dead
Friends Through Thick and Thin (with Gloria Gaither, Peggy
   Benson, and Joy MacKenzie)
Girls Gotta Have Fun!

DUH-VOTIONS

WORDS OF WISDOM FOR THE SPIRITUALLY CHALLENGED

SUE BUCHANAN

ZondervanPublishingHouse
Grand Rapids, Michigan

A Division of HarperCollinsPublishers

Duh-Votions

Copyright © 1999 by Sue Buchanan

Requests for information should be addressed to:

✚ ZondervanPublishingHouse
Grand Rapids, Michigan 49530

Library of Congress Cataloging-in-Publication Data

Buchanan, Sue.
    Duh-votions / Sue Buchanan.
    p. cm.
    ISBN 0-310-22865-4 (softcover : alk. paper)
    1. Christian women—Religious life Humor. I. Title.
BV4527.B83 1999
242'.643—dc21   99-32616
                                                                 CIP

Excerpts from *Bless This House* by Gloria Gaither. Copyright 1998 by Gloria Gaither. Used by permission of J. Countryman.

"Find Us Faithful" words and music by Jon Mohr. © 1987 Jonathan Mark Music ASCAP and Birdwing Music ASCAP. All rights reserved. Used by permission.

"Celebrating Our Diversity" © Appalachian Ministries Educational Resource Center. Used by permission.

Excerpt from *An American Childhood* by Annie Dillard, (New York: Harper & Row, 1987, p.11). Used by permission.

Published in association with the literary agency of Alive Communications, Inc., 7680 Goddard Street, Suite 200, Colorado Springs, CO 80920.

Interior design by Laura Klynstra

Printed in the United States of America

01 02 03 04 05 06 /✤ DC/ 10 9 8 7 6 5

To Mindy, Dana, and Barry

CONTENTS

INTRODUCTION

WHEN IT COMES TO daily devotions, there really are people out there who hold the Bible in front of them, let it fall open, then point and read! I'm one of those people. Don't pretend to be shocked. You bought this book!

For many years I tried to hide the fact that I'm not a spiritual giant—that I am, in fact, quite shallow. Then I wrote a book, then another (Who said you have to be deep to write a book?), and my publisher insisted I be out there speaking in order for the book to sell.

So now I'm a Christian speaker, which proves once and for all that God has a terrific sense of humor. I'm so shallow when it comes to Bible knowledge that for years I thought Solomon had 500 wives and 500 porcupines, and that Lot's wife was a pillar of salt by day and a ball of fire by night. When someone mentions the great religious author and intellectual Francis Shaeffer, I still have to ask, "Is that a man or a woman?"

Once at an Evangelical Christian Publishers' awards banquet, where all the top books in the industry are honored, I overheard this comment about the guest speaker, a prolific and well-loved author: "Well, he certainly is a better writer than he is a speaker."

Those words haunted me when I began to accept speaking dates, so I decided to tell my audience the truth right up front. I say, "I may as well tell you, because you'll figure it out anyway: I'm not that deep." They laugh. "I'm shallow." They laugh. "But I'm deep for a shallow person." They laugh again. But here's what's *really* funny! Afterward a lot of people—I'm talkin' a lot of people—come up to me and say, "I'm just like you. I'm shallow too! I've just never admitted it before."

I'm beginning to think there are more people like me than there are like *them*—and you know who the *thems* are! They are the ones who know who begot whom and can explain why the Holy Scripture insists that the " . . . meek will inherit the earth . . ."—when it seems to be the other way around.

I've not only used the "let-the-Bible-fall-open-and-point" method for my devotions, but I've been known to meditate for thirty minutes after passing one of those big neon church signs that proclaims such truths as "Do your givin' while you're livin', then you're knowin' where it's goin.'" That particular sign convinced me to hurry home and write out my check for missions. I have some sign ideas of my own, including, "Let God use you—everyone else in town has."

Sometimes I ponder spiritual truths because of something another person says or does, or because I've listened to a tape or heard a song on the radio. Sometimes I even dare call it "devotions." Perhaps the point of this book is that God can speak in unexpected ways, and you don't have to be deep to hear his voice.

With this in mind, enjoy the book (be sure to buy one for your pastor—at least half of his congregation is shallow); and if by chance a message comes through, I hope it's that God loves you no matter how deep or shallow you might be; that his message, which is about love and redemption, is so simple that even *we* (and we know who *we* are) can understand it. What he wants from us isn't all that complicated. He wants us to see him and hear his voice in the craziness of everyday life.

PERFECT DRESS, PERFECT EARRINGS, PERFECT ME

The ordinances of the LORD are sure and altogether righteous.

PSALM 19:9

I HAVE NO TROUBLE at all understanding that the Lord's ordinances are "sure and altogether righteous." I have no trouble believing that God is who he says he is, and that I'm his child because of his great plan. And I'd be willing to bet everything I own—from my Aunt Annie's Depression glass to my frog pin with the handset rhinestones—on the fact that I'll spend eternity with him.

I have no trouble at all being sure about God; it's me I can't be sure of. Some days I can't be sure of anything. Some days, even though I feel *very* sure and self-confident, I end up falling on my face.

Not long ago on a Sunday morning, I got up early and took my time getting ready. I put on my perfect new knit dress with the dramatic—I'm talking dramatic—cowl collar and the perfect matching earrings, pin, and bracelet. I happened to have the perfect shoes and even swapped out purses, which is really something for me. I prefer always to carry the big one that holds the most candy in case the sermon goes long.

This is hard to believe, but by the time I got to church I was thinking more about how perfect I was than about worshiping God. It seemed I was in luck, because just as I walked into the foyer, coming straight toward me was *the* best-dressed, *the* most fashion-conscious woman in our church; for once I felt I could hold my own—I looked good! She threw her arms wide to embrace me and I opened my arms in sweet anticipation.

"Oh Suuue! You look …" (… fabulous?… ravishing, perhaps?). Just before the moment of contact, my friend took a step backward leaving the embrace hanging in midair and me posed as though to take flight. "Do you intend to wear your dress backwards all day?"

I gathered my wits and headed to the ladies' room. Sure enough—the mirror confirmed it—hanging out over the collar, right out there in front for all to see, was the designer's label. To beat all, it wasn't a subtle, tiny, little tag. It was five inches square!

I wish I could say this is the only time I came up short in the "perfect me" department. My face turns red just thinking about the time I lost my slip when introduced at a prestigious banquet, or another time when my jacket fell open at a business meeting revealing my Victoria's secrets, or the time I wore two totally different shoes—shoes that didn't resemble each other in any way, for heaven's sake!

Then there are the times I think I'm a "perfect me" Christian and I fail. Oh, how I fail! My imperfections (and you have no idea how many there are) remind me that he is perfect, he is righteous, and that even though I don't deserve it, *I am made righteous in him!*

Dear Lord

Maybe I'll be more sure of me if I keep reminding myself of the sureness of you and your ordinances. You alone are perfect. Amen. P.S. Help me go to church for the right reasons.

YOU IN THE THIRD ROW ... STICK 'EM UP!

Hallelujah! For our Lord God Almighty reigns. Let us rejoice and be glad and give him glory! For the wedding of the Lamb has come, and his bride has made herself ready.

REVELATION 19:6–7

MY HUSBAND, WAYNE, AND I have two daughters, Dana and Mindy. Wayne and I and our two cats live in Nashville, Tennessee, in the same home—it sits like a birdhouse in the woods on a hill—we've lived in for over thirty years. Mindy resides with her two cats in a cute apartment a few miles away, and Dana is married to Barry; they live in Middletown, Ohio, where Barry heads up *InWord,* an innovative organization that creates Bible studies for teens and youth leaders. Dana is a harpist and plays for weddings almost every weekend. She always has a funny wedding-gone-awry story to tell when we all get together.

The verses from Revelation that head this chapter are, of course, about the Second Coming of Christ. Duh! Even I understand that, but I can't help thinking about all the weddings that turned into horror stories, even when the bride did everything possible to make herself ready.

Once, at the insistence of the bride, Dana played "Send in the Clowns" as the bridesmaids came down the aisle. Another time at an outdoor reception, she found that after a bathroom break, she had walked to the front of the assemblage with her dressed firmly tucked into the back of her pantyhose, her whole backside showing. The clue came when a waiter informed her, "Yo dress is in yo behind."

Another time at a candlelight service, she played while everyone was seated; then just as she began the processional, out of the corner of her eye she saw what appeared to be blue flashing lights. Just then the doors burst open and *blue uniforms* exploded into the audience, guns drawn! It seems one of the family members was wanted for a felony.

Sometimes it's the minister who needs to be arrested! My friend attended an unusual wedding. After the wedding party was in place, the minister reached under the pulpit, pulled out a Kermit-the-Frog hand puppet, and proceeded to do the whole ceremony as Kermit. At the end of the service the minister (in his own voice) said, "This is a message from God ..." and then in his Kermit voice said, "I'm here when you need me. Look me up."

It seems this was all a surprise to the bride and groom. They had arranged for a "package deal," which included a church and minister. *Sight unseen!* The church secretary who booked the event didn't mention the poor man was suffering from dementia.

My friend tells me this actually happened, and I believe it. You couldn't make up a story like that. Few weddings are that insane—that much of a horror story! Most brides are ready, and when the big day comes, it's memorable for everyone.

In most wedding albums there is a picture—near the back, next to the one of the groom's hairy hand covering the bride's perfectly manicured one—of the couple ready to take their leave. Their faces say, "Everything is perfect now and will be perfect forever." They believe it with all their hearts, and no matter how many weddings we attend, *we do too,* if only for the moment. Then at some point reality sets in.

It's pretty amazing that God uses the imagery of this most intimate of relationships to make us understand that we are being made the perfect bride for the perfect bridegroom for the perfect wedding and that, unlike an earthly marriage, reality as we know it will surely never set in. The reality is that everything will be perfect, and the intimacy will be forever!

Dear Lamb of God

It boggles my mind that you can see what we can become: your perfect bride! We don't have a clue about perfection aside from you. Your wedding will be perfect. Make us ready. "Hallelujah! For our Lord God Almighty reigns." Amen.

YOU'LL FIND THE FRUIT OF THE SPIRIT IN PLASTIC BAGS HANGING FROM THE LUGGAGE CART

*But the fruit of the Spirit is love, joy, peace,
patience, kindness, goodness, faithfulness,
gentleness and self-control.*

GALATIANS 5:22–23

I DO A PRETTY good job of living out the fruit of the Spirit, even if I do say so myself—at least eight fruits out of nine isn't bad! It's the "self-control fruit" that I have trouble with. I suppose when you get right down to it, having no self-control can pretty much erase the good you've accomplished in living out the others. Sometimes it's like my spirit is an out-of-control bus. Or luggage cart, maybe!

Gloria Gaither, Peggy Benson, Joy MacKenzie, and I had just finished speaking at a "Friends Through Thick and Thin" seminar in Mississippi. We'd had one of our best weekends ever. We had made a strong connection with several hundred warm, open women, and there was no doubt the presence of God had been there and had moved in all our hearts.

We'd also had a raucous good time as a foursome. We stayed in a brand-new, small, comfortable, suite hotel, and the host committee had lavished us with baskets of fruit, cheese, crackers, juices, and sweets.

We hated to leave each other, but Gloria had a plane to catch. The plan was that we would pack up, and Peg, Joy, and I (who were driving home) would drop Gloria off at the airport on our way out of town.

There was no bell hop, so we found a big luggage carrier and loaded it with all our stuff: leftover boxes of books, garment bags, suitcases, carry-ons, purses, book bags, shoe boxes, and pillows. Hanging from each end were two plastic laundry bags, fat with the leftover goodies—one for the van and one for Gloria to take on the plane.

When we pushed through the lobby, you couldn't tell there was a luggage cart, just this pile of "stuff" on wheels—a pile of stuff that seemed to include a stuck pig, considering the way it squealed.

When we got the cart to the van, Peg, Gloria, and I felt our job was pretty much finished. We knew from experience that packing the trunk is Joy's thing, and it's best to stand back and get out of her way. Heaven forbid you should hand her something before she has a place for it!

With the pressure off, I guess you could say we relaxed. We just kinda folded our arms, drifted into la-la land, and waited for Joy (on her haunches in the rear of the van) to give directions.

I'm not sure when it registered, whether it was when we saw the look of terror on Joy's face, or when we realized the noise we were hearing—the faint little clicking sound that grew in intensity until it became the sound of a stuck pig trying to get out of town—but the next thing we knew, there went our cart flying down the hill.

We just stood there paralyzed, watching our belongings picking up speed—practically becoming airborne—and heading toward a four-lane street. From my vantage point, I could see we'd lucked out; nothing was coming in either direction. Across the road, however, I could see a curb and in my mind's eye I could envision the cart, going ninety miles an hour, hitting it, exploding into the air, and disappearing into the great beyond! Our possessions would be in heaven with the Lord before we would!

Fortunately the cart changed its mind (possibly when the wheel fell off) and made a little zig, then a zag, a left turn, then went end over end and landed upside down in a ditch of rich, thick, red Mississippi mud. Somehow we managed to collect (and clean up) our belongings and get them packed into the van, even though we were convulsing with laughter. We made a very reluctant Gloria take the poor, bent-up cart with two broken wheels inside to the desk, apologize, and offer to pay. Speaking of self-control (we were, weren't we?), we all had to make a fast dash to the rest room and a faster dash to the airport.

Dear Lord

I'm like a runaway luggage cart when it comes to self-control. Give me love, joy, peace, patience, kindness, goodness, faithfulness, and gentleness, yes! But for heaven's sake, give me that elusive thing called self-control. It seems I'm always having to clean up the mud from my life. Be the God of my every pilgrimage. Amen.

IF A COW LAUGHED, WOULD MILK COME OUT HER NOSE?

*There is a time for everything, and a season
for every activity under heaven: . . . a time to
weep and a time to laugh.*

ECCLESIASTES 3:1, 4

ALL MY LIFE PEOPLE have reminded me that there's a time to laugh and a time to shut up; I didn't even know it was in the Bible. Duh! It seems I'm always laughing at the wrong time or at the wrong thing. I somehow think that when conversation gets too heavy—too serious—it's up to me to lighten things up. This gets me into trouble.

This book, of course, is the outgrowth of a warped personality. And it's no wonder I'm warped! From the time I was a small child, my parents would look at me as though I was from Mars, shake their heads at each other, and one of them would mutter, "She's not like my side of the family!" to which the other would respond, "Well, she's certainly not like my side, either!" I wasn't a bad child; I was just unpredictable, and I saw humor in everything.

When I was older it seemed perfectly acceptable to my parents that I would go to college to meet people and have a good time–and have a good time, I did! Perhaps it was the day and age in which I grew up, and education for girls wasn't as important as it is now. Perhaps my parents were dealing in reality!

Then I married Wayne, and in the early years of our marriage, we found ourselves surrounded by more than our share of what I call "Tsk, Tsk-ers"–those people who seem to be against more things than they are for. During those years, the unspoken disclaimer–"She's not like our side of the family"–hurt me deeply, because the family in question seemed to me to be the family of God.

Fortunately, Wayne had a great sense of humor too, and when we would find ourselves in uptight company (and there seemed to be a lot of that going around at the time), a twinkle would pass from his eyes to mine, and I knew I could make it through the day, or evening, or even the rest of my life! Often at the end of the day, I could let my hair down and poke fun at the things that had amused me. One acquaintance, who was quite pompous but not too clean in her bodily habits, became "Lady Slop Jar," and I could imitate her perfectly, much to Wayne's amusement.

There isn't enough space in this book to tell of the times I felt out of place–like an alien on a strange planet. Then we moved to Nashville. Once here, we fell in with a group of friends who were almost as crazy as we were; and even if they weren't quite as crazy as I was, they let me be *me*. They "celebrated" me being me!

As a video producer and show producer, again I had permission to be "me." "She's creative!" they said. "Creative people are different." So whether I showed up for a very formal meeting on Wall Street shouting, "Howdy!" and passing out Minnie Pearl fans to everyone, or on the island of Bonaire at midnight jumped into the ocean while still wearing my fancy dinner clothes, folks simply laughed and said, "Consider the source."

Sometimes I have "partners in crime." Several years ago, we were in a restaurant with friends. We had just ordered dessert when one of the men (famous for the size of his appetite) went to the rest room. While he was gone we soaked a paper napkin in milk and put it under the crust of his cherry pie. When he came back, he ate every bite, all the while saying he'd never had better pie. We couldn't stop laughing and our guffaws were loud and obnoxious, causing other customers to complain. It wasn't that it wasn't "a time to laugh," it was that we were doing it too loudly and infringing on the privacy of others.

Sometimes I laugh alone. Just recently there were several of us around the dinner table and Gloria, who is a John Steinbeck scholar, was enthusiastically discussing his writings. To me, the conversation had been too serious too long, so I took it upon myself to loosen things up. "I like Steinway," I said, "he has really good pianos." It was obvious that my timing was off. Let me just say that if looks could kill, I'd be dead.

Not long ago, I was waiting to board a plane when I noticed the cutest little old dried-up couple—eighty if they were a day. You could tell by their nervousness they weren't in the habit of flying. When the flight was called they picked up their old-fashioned satchel, taped-up cardboard box, shopping bag, coats, and sweaters, and got in line.

All the way out the jetway the woman, who happened to be walking next to me, kept up a stream of chatter. I thought perhaps she was talking to herself, that maybe she was senile. Then I realized she thought her husband was behind her and she was talking to him. Somehow he had dropped behind, and another man had gotten between them. Just as we got to the door of the plane she gave a big exasperated exclamation, like the sound of a train engine letting off steam, and said, "Answer me, you old fool!" Without looking, she swung her carry-on around (with more power than you would expect from a professional boxer) and hit, not her short little husband, but the very tall man behind her in the absolute worst possible part of his anatomy imaginable. The poor man dropped his belongings, grabbed his lower parts, bent double, and let out the most pitiful—like-that-of-childbirth—groan you've ever heard.

This time I almost got thrown off the plane. I laughed all the way to Dallas. This time it was I who was suspected of being senile.

Dear God

You, being God, could have said, "There will be no laughter—period." I'm glad you didn't. You said there is a time for everything, and a season for every activity . . . a time to weep and a time to laugh. Help me know when and where. Give me sensitivity, but don't let me lose the joy of living. Amen.

FISHIN' POLES AND NIGHT CRAWLERS

*He has taken me to the banquet hall, and
his banner over me is love.*

SONG OF SONGS 2:4

MY HUSBAND GAVE ME a gift a while back. He said, "It will come
as a surprise when you least expect it." I don't like to wait. I want
my presents now (and *later too*, now that I think of it). I was
hoping for another one of those lovely little hand-set scatter pins
with the Austrian crystals he is so fond of giving me. I practiced
what I would say: "Oh, another butterfly (. . . or turtle . . . or
bumblebee). Thank you. *You shouldn't have!"*

It turned out that Wayne's gift to me *did* come as a surprise,
even after the warning. It didn't glitter as I'd hoped, but I must
say, it certainly has become a bright spot in my day. One morning when I logged on to my e-mail, I found my gift: a subscrip-
tion to A.Word.A.Day! Right at the top of the screen it said:
"From: wsmith@wordsmith.org, To: [Are you ready for this?]
linguaphile!" *Me! A linguaphile!*

I had no idea what it meant, but it certainly sounded impressive. I quickly found out Mr. Webster didn't know either. Linguaphile isn't in the dictionary, not even in the unabridged dictionary! However, if you look up "lingua" you'll find it means "of the tongue," and "phile," when added to a noun or adjective, means "loving." Put the two together and—unless you think a linguaphile is someone who loves his tongue—you have to believe it's a newfangled word coined to mean "a lover of the words that come off the tongue." I buy that!

But me a linguaphile? It was all I could do to keep from calling my friends. "Hey, Gloria, I don't want to brag, but I thought you'd like to know, I'm a linguaphile."

What an accolade for someone who never read a real honest-to-goodness book till she was thirty years old! Oh, I read (skimmed) the necessary assignments for high school and college, and I read *How to Win Friends and Influence People* because my father insisted, but I'm talking about sitting down with a good book and savoring it. I'm sorry to say I didn't do that.

Now I not only read books, but I write them, and I can't help wondering if I might have become an author sooner if my tenth-grade teacher hadn't held my creative writing paper high above her head and ridiculed it in front of the class. "A tenth-grader didn't write this," she said. "It's too good; it's plagiarized!" Because this was a time in history when you kept your mouth shut and didn't argue, and because I was embarrassed out of my mind, I never said a word. And I never wrote again till I was forty-five years old! Now I revel in the fact I'm a linguaphile, as each day I go to my e-mail and find my new word, its pronunciation, its meaning, what part of speech it is, and a sentence that uses it properly.

For a while I sent e-mail to Wayne using each new word in a sentence of my own. "Dear Wayne, I hope you get to practice your ichthyology (study of fishes) before the week is over." (Wayne's study of fish requires a fishing pole and some night crawlers.) Another thing I did was try, as much as possible, to use each new word in conversation throughout the day. Some days, try as I may, it's impossible, like in the case of the word "earwig," which means: "Any of various elongate insects of the order Dermaptera, having a pair of pincerlike appendages protruding from the rear of the abdomen." Sounds painful to me!

Believe it or not—and don't forget this book is about finding God in the craziness of everyday life—sometimes this Word.A.Day is a message straight from him. Take this morning. The word is "oriflamme," and it's a noun. Its meaning: "A banner. An inspiring standard or symbol."

I wonder if it's a coincidence that the words I read in Scripture today are "He has taken me to the banquet hall, and his banner over me is love"? Maybe so, but perhaps he's making sure that I understand this banner thing. Pounding it into my head, so to speak. I'm struck by the fact that God often uses something mundane to drive home his message. He knows me well; he knows how intrigued I am by new words, how I love to use them—try them out! Okay, here goes: His oriflamme is waving over me!

Dear God

Help me not write it off as coincidence when you speak to me in unexpected ways; may I not take your words for granted. Thank you for your banner that waves over me, and that the banner is love *because . . . "love is patient, love is kind. It does not envy, it does not boast, it is not proud. It is not rude, it is not self-seeking, it is not easily angered, it keeps no record of wrongs. Love does not delight in evil but rejoices with the truth. It always protects, always trusts, always hopes, always perseveres. Love never fails" (1 Corinthians 13:4–8). Amen.*

A CLEAR CONSCIENCE IS USUALLY THE SIGN OF A BAD MEMORY

. . . a nagging spouse is a leaky faucet.
PROVERBS 19:13 (THE MESSAGE)

EUGENE PETERSON, WHO PARAPHRASED the Bible into contemporary language, really knows how to bring it right down to the nitty-gritty. Sometimes I can ignore the nicety-nice words of other versions, then read the same passage in *The Message,* and it just kind of slams me against the wall with its visual images. How could you ignore (or forget) the analogy of a leaky faucet?

Not that I've ever nagged. I have a clear conscience about that. I'm just saying in case I was ever *tempted* to nag, this image of a dripping faucet would stop me immediately.

We've had fire trucks screaming through our neighborhood in the middle of the night and slept right through it (according to our neighbors), but I doubt we've ever slept through a dripping faucet.

"Hear that?"

"Your turn to get it."

"Uh-uh. Your turn. Besides, whoever mentions it first has to get it."

"I think I can sleep through it."

SFX (which in a video script means *sound effects*): *Stumble, stumble; mumble, mumble; grumble, grumble.*

"Snore!"

If women quit nagging entirely, men would have nothing to complain about. Where would they get their jokes?

My parents had close friends who bantered continually. She nagged. He complained.

"Aren't you wearing your wedding ring on the wrong finger?" she would say. "Yes, I am; I married the wrong woman."

"You know, I was a fool when I married you."

"Yes dear, but I was in love then and didn't notice."

I was grown before I realized they were doing a comedy routine and enjoying every minute of it. And loved each other! They were a regular George Burns and Gracie Allen, and I almost missed it.

Okay, so I've nagged! I dare say, so have you! Let's try something. I will if you will. What if every time we were tempted to nag we would instead go into the bathroom, shut the door, and pray for deliverance? No, I have a better idea! What if we would go into the bathroom, shut the door, turn on the faucet to a drip, sit down on the throne, and *listen*? Maybe give it thirty minutes or so. Sit there and just listen. Listen to that hateful, disturbing, nerve-wracking, annoying, horrible, despicable, IRRITATING, DISGUSTING, DRIVE-YOU-CRAZY, IN-YOUR-FACE DRRRIPPING FAAUUCCEETT! EEEeek!

I needed that. I think I'm cured!

Dear Lord

> *Dear God: If—I'm just saying if—I should ever be tempted to nag my husband, please remind me again of the leaky faucet. Amen.*

I NEVER WOULD HAVE LIED, LORD, IF IT HADN'T BEEN COUNTRY MUSIC WEEK

Each of you must put off falsehood and speak truthfully to his neighbor, for we are all members of one body.

EPHESIANS 4:25

WE HAVE TWO CATS, Dizzy and Jazz. Dizzy is, in fact, slightly dizzy. The truth is, she's more than just dizzy. She's as dumb as a wall—just a notch above a crustacean—but we love her. Jazz is smart. She can talk, although I'm pretty much the only one who has heard her do it. When she wants out, she meows in such a way that it sounds very much like "out." When she wants food, her meow sounds altogether different. It sounds like "eat." When she wants to be petted, she does an impression of a mouse. She squeaks.

Neither of our cats are any special breed. I suppose both could be called alley cats, but only in the broad sense of the word, since neither has ever seen an alley. Sometimes we say that Jazz is a "Muldavian gray," just to make her think she's special.

The Muldavian gray thing started once when we hired a man from Chicago to come to Nashville to consult with our company. Wayne and I are partners in a company called Dynamic Media. We specialize in video, interactive computer presentations, Internet services, and corporate meetings. Because it was Country Music Week, all the hotels were full and we invited this man to stay at our house. As I was showing him to his room, Jazz brushed against his legs, and he bent down to pet her. "Oh, she's just beautiful. What kind of cat is she?" he asked. "Some exotic breed?"

"Matter of fact, she is," I answered. "She's a Muldavian gray."

I know this is hard to believe, but I have no idea where that answer came from. It just popped into my head and out of my mouth! I suppose I thought—if I was thinking at all—that he would know I was joking and we would share a good laugh over the fact there really is no such thing as a Muldavian gray. But it was too late. My joke was backfiring terribly.

"Oh, I love Muldavian grays. They are my favorite!" he said, and he didn't stop with that. He kept going, I guess trying to impress me with his profound knowledge of the feline kingdom—pouring it on—and I didn't have the heart to stop him! He said that Jazz was one of the finest specimens of that particular breed he'd ever seen.

I kept waiting for the glimmer in his eye, waiting for him to crack up over the fact he had actually pulled one over on me, instead of the other way around. *Soon we'll be poking each other in the ribs*, I was thinking. *Surely he's joking*. But he wasn't. He was serious, and I couldn't bring myself to tell him the truth. I simply showed him where his towels were, explained that there was extra toilet paper under the sink. Then I hightailed it up the stairs.

The next morning I found our guest on his prayer rug, chanting to a deity never before (or since) worshiped in our home; since I had not spoken *truthfully* the night before, somehow I couldn't bring myself to witness about my faith.

Dear Lord

Help me to speak truthfully. *It's not always easy—like in the case of the cat, which was intended to be a joke. Amen. P.S. The cat doesn't really talk, but is it okay if I just pretend she does?*

ONE PERSON'S ART IS
ANOTHER PERSON'S JUNK

*Make a careful exploration of who you are
and the work you have been given, and then
sink yourself into that. Don't be impressed
with yourself. Don't compare yourself with
others. Each of you must take responsibility
for doing the creative best you can with your
own life.*

GALATIANS 6:4–5 (THE MESSAGE)

TO "MAKE A CAREFUL exploration of who I am" would be to take a trip back to Charleston, West Virginia, where I was born and raised, where I grew up in a society in which you were either rich or poor. The middle class was a very small segment of the population. I went to school with kids who had no shoes unless the state provided them, and I went home to spend the night with girls who shared a bedroom with six or eight or even ten brothers and sisters. Some of them lived in three-room shacks with front porches that sagged so steeply beneath the weight of washing machines, refrigerators, car motors, and other miscellaneous junk that we could play "slicky slide" on the incline.

Even though my father was a successful businessman, my parents were not "class-conscious." They had dinner at the governor's mansion on occasion and mixed with the elite. We sometimes had dinner at the home of a very proper and very rich old dowager, and I learned at an early age to use a finger bowl properly. I tell you this, so that if you should invite me to a fancy-schmantzy dinner party and put out your finger bowls, you can be confident I won't embarrass you by drinking the water.

A year or so ago, I spoke in Kentucky for an insurance company. Afterward one of the women hung around till I finished doing a television interview. She was an old classmate, and we spent the afternoon talking each other's legs off. As we reminisced about our childhood, it dawned on us that, in a way, we had lived *Coal Miner's Daughter,* the life story of country music star Loretta Lynn—a movie that had deeply moved each of us. It closely portrayed the living conditions of many of our young friends.

"I had no idea they were poor," said my childhood friend Margaret, and as though thoroughly surprised at the thought she added, "Compared to them we were wealthy! Did you know?"

I shook my head. Truthfully! I had had no idea!

To "explore who I am as a Christian" would be to go back to a little cinder block fundamentalist church in West Virginia—a church that seemingly did everything wrong. They had a rule for everything. We were told "godly women" didn't dance, or smoke, or chew ("Chew," you ask? Remember, we're talking West Virginia here!), or go to movies, or play cards. And godly women certainly didn't wear makeup! At the time, I figured someday I'd be godly when I was old and gray. Now I know as long as Clairol stays in business I'll never be gray!

One thing they were doing right in that little church, however, was treasuring God's Word, and they believed you should memorize it—"hide it in your heart." As kids, Scripture was pounded into our heads, and thus my identity as a Christian became real over a lifetime, as biblical truths played out and I found them to be true and trustworthy.

(Back to the verse!) I don't think I'm very impressed with myself (except maybe when I've made a perfect chocolate pie or hit *just right* with the deviled eggs), and I try not to compare myself to others anymore. How different I am from most of my friends. The way I dress, how I do my hair, the way I decorate our house—my mother called it Gypsy—so many things! It took me a long time to understand that God didn't make a mistake when he made me; he did it *on purpose!*

Doing "the creative best" with my life is something to think about. I have some weird ideas! For instance—you'll think me tasteless, but—I've always loved *yard art*. Most people turn their noses up at it, but I'm told it's making a comeback. Garden shops are popping up everywhere, and they are full of everything from birdbaths to St. Christopher statues to garden rocks that say things such as, "God's Handiwork" and "Grow, Darn It!" The problem is, I love it all—in the same yard!

Not long ago, I was in a la-dee-da shop in Dallas and, lo and behold, there among the pink flamingos on a birdbath pedestal was one of those iridescent globes like the ones fortune tellers use. In West Virginia where I grew up, we thought they were BB gun targets! The shopkeeper told us, "It's the latest thing."

You could say I'd waited a lifetime for this moment. After all, being from the hills, I thought a rusted old washing machine was yard art!

My parents called it "yard *junk*." I'll never forget driving through those hollows on a Sunday afternoon and hearing them comment on the sights. They had come from Ohio as newlyweds, moving into a home given them by my grandfather as a wedding present. My grandfather had been a railroader with the New York Central and had a good eye for property investments before times got hard. Mama and Daddy never quite got over being surprised at the ways of the hillbilly. I was born there, so I never knew the difference.

Anything that had been won at the carnival seemed to be yard-appropriate. There were plaster of Paris dogs, cats, frogs, alligators, and every character from Snow White and the Seven Dwarfs, some with their heads severed and lying in the grass beside their bodies, looking like casualties of war. My favorites were Kewpie dolls—squatty little dolls that were fat-cheeked at both ends—painted the most electric colors imaginable.

There were countless birdhouses on skinny poles towering almost to heaven proclaiming, "See Rock City," and herd after herd of fake reindeer whose painted-on eyes were so real they haunted my dreams! An ancient kettle or wash tub turned upside-down became a plant stand. Right-side-up, voila! A flower pot. Stuck in the ground it was a small pond. Spinning a useless, frenzied dervish were whirligigs—all sizes, all shapes, all colors. Colorful flower gardens were everywhere planted in discarded sinks, bathtubs, and even an occasional commode. On our Sunday soirees, we saw such interesting things—sometimes all in the same front yard!

And what they did with old tires! There would be whole yards full, each one overflowing with flowers. Some were painted bright colors, turned upright, and partially imbedded in the ground; no real reason for their existence except to create . . . shall we call it "ambiance"? And to think it's all coming back!

God of flowers and gardens and beauty: And people! All different! All unique! You are truly a God of creativity! Let us not compare our differences; let us celebrate our differences! Thank you for who I am! Crazy me! Thank you for the life lessons I learned growing up in West Virginia and for the Scripture I learned in spite of myself. Thank you that I can count on that Scripture, can live by it! Amen.

YOU GIVE ME BIG TIP, I GIVE YOU FANCY NAIL

*Your beauty should not come from outward
adornment, such as braided hair and the
wearing of gold jewelry and fine clothes.
Instead, it should be that of your inner self,
the unfading beauty of a gentle and quiet
spirit, which is of great worth in God's sight.*

1 PETER 3:3–4

I'VE NEVER BRAIDED MY hair, but I certainly have had a French twist piled up to the sky, held by a big old tortoise-shell comb with pearls as big as quarters. Matter of fact, I've had more than one hairdo ruined by a ceiling fan!

As for gold jewelry, my question to God would be, *"Define* gold jewelry, and does the definition include *faux* gold jewelry?" There is no mention in that verse of long, manicured, painted fingernails. It might have been an oversight, but I see it as a loophole!

A few days before Christmas last year I went to my regular nail girl for a fill-in and polish. She's a darling Vietnamese woman who knows only a few words of English, every one of which she used that day to try to convince me to let her paint Christmas decorations on my nails.

Her musical Asian voice seemed to span an octave. "Sooo pret-teee," she said, gesturing to the samples on the wall. She gave a little pout when I didn't nod my agreement.

"I have a couple of business meetings and I can't possibly *show up* with a manger scene spread across ten nails," I snapped, knowing she wouldn't understand a word. (They didn't *really* offer a manger scene.)

"Shooow up," she smiled. "Yes, shooow up."

A couple of days later, I broke a nail. It was Christmas Eve, but fortunately the shop was open and my sweet friend greeted me with a big smile. "Shooow up," she said.

"Fix nail," I said, holding up my index finger. I could see the disappointment in her eyes. I'm positive she thought I came back for the manger scene.

I was feeling the spirit of the season, so when the job was finished—after all it was Christmas Eve—I handed her a five-dollar tip.

"Oh, toooo much teep, toooo much teep," she squealed as she grabbed my hand back. "You geeve me toooo much teep. I geeve you fahn-cy nail."

"No! No fahn-cy nail! No want fahn-cy nail." (When did I live in Vietnam?) I tried my best to retrieve my hand. Too late! She was already at work. Her stunning black eyes danced as she airbrushed a Christmas tree, truly a work of art, while I tried (in two languages and three religions, for heaven's sake!) to convince her this wasn't my thing.

The Christmas tree on my pointer finger turned out to be quite a conversation piece—*as if my friends need a conversation piece!* I like that about my friends, and I like the fact that you don't have to apologize for who you are or what you think. You can discuss anything and everything and know you won't be judged. You can have a Christmas tree painted on your fingernail and your friends will say, "How like our Sue. She's nuts, but we love her!"

When Gloria, Peggy, Joy, and I wrote the book *Friends Through Thick and Thin* and then began to travel together, we realized how very different we are in every way. Two of us are messy in hotel rooms and two are neat. Two have impressive credentials when it comes to education. Two don't. One didn't go to college at all but instead got married and had babies (her grandchildren are her credentials); and one went to college to meet guys! Guess who!

The four of us even look different. Very different! One looks like a cute grandma with long corduroy dresses and granny boots. One looks like the school teacher she is in tailored suits and blouses and comfortable shoes. One wears flowing chiffons in bright colors. And the other one, they say is always overdressed, her skirts are much too short, her heels too high, and her earrings too big. (To find out who is who, please go right out and buy the book!)

While I admire the outward beauty of Gloria, Peggy, and Joy (and other close friends), the thing that draws me to them and keeps me holding on for dear life is that each of them possesses an inner beauty that comes from knowing God intimately. Their true beauty comes from being deeply rooted in him, and their quest for a deeper knowledge of his precepts compels me to dwell more on my inner self rather than on the outward appearance.

Dear Lord

God of gentle and quiet spirits: I understand exactly what you're saying about beauty—that it doesn't come from artificial things. Let me align myself with friends who possess a beauty of spirit. Let it rub off on me! *How I long for a gentle and quiet spirit. I long to please you. Amen.*

DO ANGELS REALLY WEAR UNDERWEAR?

*Do not forget to entertain strangers, for by
so doing some people have entertained angels
without knowing it.*

HEBREWS 13:2

WHEN I READ HEBREWS 13:2 the first time I thought it said, "Do not forget to entertain strange people," and my reaction was, "I do it all the time. Most of my guests are strange." When my husband reads that verse, he never fails to bring up the fact that years ago there was a book titled *Angel Unaware* and that he thought the title was *Angel's Underwear.*

Wayne and I love to entertain. We learned the art from my parents. No one did it better. As we stood by Daddy's casket with tears streaming down our faces, I'll never forget someone asking, "Did anyone think to get Maynard's [yes, it really was his name] recipe for cheese dip?"

When I think of my childhood home, I remember wonderful smells wafting their way from the kitchen. Usually there were sounds coming from there too. Laughter, giggles, and yes, even squeals. My parents loved being in the kitchen together. Mother, who always looked perfect in her high-heeled shoes and starched house dresses with their pinched-in waists, was known for being a good cook; her specialty was pie: pumpkin, coconut cream, chocolate, strawberry, rhubarb; the list goes on. Daddy liked cooking too and was known for throwing all the leftovers in the skillet, adding eggs, and cooking up what he called his "mess." I used to say that I left home to get away from that Sunday night fare; but if the truth be known, it was my favorite.

Until I was in junior high school we lived in a darling little three-bedroom cottage on a tree-lined street. It had a front porch with a swing and a glider where the neighbors loved to gather. The living room and dining room were connected by a wide French door that opened to make one large room out of the two. I remember hearing my parents say that if and when they moved, they'd like the same floor plan because "it can hold a lot of people."

My playhouse under the back porch held a lot of people too—all the kids in the neighborhood! And just like my parents, I was known for my hospitality. I would dress up in my mother's old clothes: a lace blouse that dragged on the floor, high-heeled shoes, a hat with a brim out to there, gloves, jewels, and an animal around my neck that bit its own tail. I was known for my pies, too—mud pies!

Sure enough, when my family moved to a bigger house, the prerequisite was met: a living room and dining room that connected and held "a lot of people." Not only did my parents throw parties with great panache, but they were always having church groups over and inviting people home for Sunday dinner. If anyone had the gift of hospitality, *they* did.

When my brother Joe and I were children (Jon was yet to be born), Daddy was in the shoe business and worked alongside a young Jewish woman who had a favorite Yiddish expression, which she used freely behind the backs of her customers. She used it to express total frustration; translated it meant "hole in

the head." Naturally, everyone picked up on it. Daddy even
taught two-year-old Joe to say it.

My father frequently brought home business associates from
out of town who "needed a good home-cooked meal." One night
he brought a strange little curmudgeon of a man who, without
even a "hello," began to dance around the dining room table
with great animation, pointing to each dish and questioning
Mama in great detail as to its ingredients. When he seemed to
have resolved some food-related issues that only he was party to,
he reached in his pocket and pulled out what appeared to us to
be a black beanie. With great flourish, he plopped it on his head,
sat down, and began to eat. We were flabbergasted! He didn't
even wait for Daddy to ask the blessing! We'd never seen such
a thing! At the time, we knew very little about the Jewish faith,
and I doubt he'd given a fleeting thought to ours.

Joe watched in amazement from the vantage point of his
high chair until he could restrain himself no longer. You should
have seen the look on our guest's face—*yes, he was Jewish and no,
my brother couldn't possibly have known*—when Joe gleefully clapped
his hands and in perfect Yiddish blurted out: "hole in the head!"

This man may not have been an angel, but my guess is that
because of sheer numbers, we did, in fact, entertain a few angels.
Many of our guests blessed our lives beyond words, and the
blessing continues to this very day.

Not long ago Dana and Barry bought their first home, and
Wayne and I couldn't wait to spend a long weekend helping
them whip it into shape. I knew we were delivering several
rooms of wallpaper we'd bought in Nashville, but I had no idea
Wayne, who hasn't wallpapered in years, intended to actually *do*
the papering. He was sure he could get the big kitchen done and
maybe even the master bedroom. Perhaps a bathroom. "It's like
riding a horse," he said. "You never forget!"

Never let it be said I'd question my husband's judgment, but
I practically choked. "He's crazy!" I mouthed to my daughter.
"He can't do that."

"Crazy as a loon!" she whispered. And what can I say? We were right! At least partially right. After huffing and puffing up and down the ladder for a solid fourteen hours (and practically pasting himself to the wall a couple of times), Wayne finished the kitchen and magnanimously announced he'd be happy to pay to have the rest done so we didn't have to work the whole time and could have more quality time together. Oh yeah, sure! *So that he didn't have to end up in the hospital in traction for a month!*

After the house was in order we invited Barry's family, the Shafers; his sister and her family, the McCollums; and good friends, the Millers, for a party. Dana and I made fudge pies and whipped fresh cream. I decorated the bay window with poinsettias and candles (it was Christmas time), Barry polished the silver, and Dana and Wayne set out the Lenox. The guests arrived laden with goodies: Barry's grandma with her well-loved carrot cake, his mother, Bonnie, with her famous apple pie, and his sister Becky with cookies for the kids. Barry built a fire with wood from the generous supply on the back porch—a house-warming gift from the Millers.

We ate and laughed and took a tour of the house, at last gathering close around the fireplace. Wayne read Gloria Gaither's book *Bless This House,* which reads in part:

> For those who stay, may the warmth of the memories created here be a comfort and a shelter from the fears of the unknown.
>
> May all the seasons be celebrated here—summer, fall, spring, and winter.
>
> May these mantels and doorways, tables and porches, be decorated with dogwood and pussy willows, flowers and fruit, bittersweet and pumpkins, berries and pine.
>
> Let there be feasting and dancing . . . laughter and games!
>
> May candlelight flicker and instruments play and voices harmonize.

May this house be a place of celebration because hearts are filled with gratitude for the gift of each new day.

That night as we compared notes on families, I was struck by the fact that Barry and Dana come from a long line of people who possessed (and possess) the gift of hospitality. We found that on both sides of the family, "the gift" includes being available and making our homes available for a celebration of many or for the solace of a single lonely soul. Dana and Barry come from hospitable people, those Shafers, Swartzes, Davises, and Buchanans!

Dear Lord

Thank you for guests who have come to our house to enjoy Wayne's spectacular chicken andaluza and fabulous flan and my famous deviled eggs (famous because I'm the only one who makes them anymore), coconut cream pie (just like Mama's), and baked Alaska (not all these things at once). Thank you, too, for those who have sat around the kitchen table with us and passed the peanut butter jar and the knife as well—satisfied just that we are together! Amen.

AND DON'T GO INTO MR. MCGREGOR'S GARDEN

A good name is more desirable than great riches; to be esteemed is better than silver or gold.

PROVERBS 22:1

PROVERBS 22:1 IS A *Duh!* for me. In fact, I always reminded my children of it as they left the house. I didn't say those exact words, but my girls certainly knew what I meant when I said, "Don't forget whose kid you are," or, "Don't go into Mr. McGregor's garden," which is what my mother said to me when I was a kid. It was her way of saying, "Behave yourself!" and it referred, of course, to the story of Peter Rabbit. We certainly know about *him* and the way he disobeyed his mama, squeezing under the gate and stuffing himself with all the vegetables his tummy could hold till he was "feeling rather sick."

We know about the chase scene that ensued, the gooseberry net that stripped him of his fine jacket with the brass buttons, the friendly sparrows, the big scary sieve, the tool shed, the watering can, the sneeze that just about got him caught, the mouse that was no help at all, the garden gate, and finally having to go home and face his mama in disgrace.

Peter Rabbit obviously came from a long line of rabbits who were expected to do the right thing, to obey and certainly not get into the kind of trouble he did.

If Proverbs 22:1 doesn't get to you, the *Tale of Peter Rabbit* will!

Not long ago a woman we knew died, and I heard someone say, "I'll bet she left a large estate." Well, that's not really what was said; what was said was, "I'll bet she left a bundle!" I doubt I'll leave behind a "bundle," but I sure wouldn't mind leaving enough for my kids to have a nice trip to Hawaii and an oil change. More than that, I'd like to leave "a good name," a heritage of faithfulness, an example of a believer for generations to come.

Find Us Faithful

We're pilgrims on the journey of the narrow road,
And those who've gone before us line the way.
Cheering on the faithful,
Encouraging the weary,
Their lives a stirring testament to God's sustaining grace.

Surrounded by so great a cloud of witnesses,
Let us run the race not only for the prize;
But as those who've gone before us,
Let us leave to those behind us
The heritage of faithfulness passed on through godly lives.

O may all who come behind us find us faithful,
May the fire of our devotion light their way.
May the footprints that we leave
Lead them to believe
And the lives we live inspire them to obey.
O may all who come behind us find us faithful.

After all our hopes and dreams have come and gone,
And our children sift through all we've left behind,
May the clues that they discover
And the memories they uncover

Become the light that leads them to the road we
       each must find.

O may all who come behind us find us faithful,
May the fire of our devotion light their way.
May the footprints that we leave
Lead them to believe
And the lives we live inspire them to obey.
O may all who come behind us find us faithful.

Dear Lord

*Remind me of how responsible I am, dear God, when it comes
to your good Name. Remind me every day of who I am—your
child. Thank you for a rich, rich heritage. For those without
that godly heritage, help them to understand* that it can begin
now, *so that years from now their progenitors will say proudly,
"I come from a long line of people who obeyed God. I have a
rich heritage." Amen.*

THE SUMMER OF MY DISCONTENTMENT

Keep your lives free from the love of money
and be content with what you have, because
God has said, "Never will I leave you;
never will I forsake you."

HEBREWS 13:5

THIS IS A VERY bad time to be reminded of Hebrews 13:5. The word that jumps out here is "content." Most of the time, I'm quite content with what I have, but occasionally, *like this very week,* content I am not.

If I'd never started redecorating Dana's old room, it never would have become the summer of my discontentment. I was happy with that room for at least twenty-five years, the last ten of which we called it "the junk room." It's been a perfect place for me to pack and unpack and not even put the suitcase away if I didn't feel like it—or the clothes for that matter.

Jewelry hung from lamps and picture frames, scarves were draped over doorknobs and dresser pulls. There were a couple of hats stuck haphazardly on the wall, and silk and lace nighties decorated the four-poster bed.

You might think the room sounds interesting until I tell you about the big gross black clothes hamper that was right there in plain open sight. And the cat box. And the basket that held a year's supply of kitty litter. Then there was the yellow shag carpet—*ugly* yellow shag carpet!

My discontentment began with a swatch of material, and now it's like a freight train that won't stop! I'm anything but content! The painter hasn't called back; the carpet man, who did come when he was supposed to, is calling daily to find out when I want the carpet, which I don't, of course, because the painting isn't done yet.

When the painter didn't come, Wayne suggested we drywall the ceiling to cover up the blown-on ceiling that was there. Enter Nacho and PePe!

I don't know the word for ceiling in Spanish so I point upward and blurt out the first thing that comes to my mind: "¿Aqui es su perro?" which translates, "Where is your dog?" "¿Mi perro?" asks Nacho with a puzzled look. "¿Yo quiero Taco Bell?" I reply. They aren't laughing; they look at me like I'm *muy loco*.

The chair and footstool have to be loaded in the station wagon and taken to the upholsterer. I have to decide on the window treatment, measure the window, and drag that big bolt of material (and the duvet that needs covering) to the sewing lady.

And I'm second-guessing myself, which is, I suppose, a form of discontentment. The good news is I paid only a hundred and eighty-five dollars for forty yards of fabric. The bad news is it's big bold magnolias on a black background, and I may have gotten carried away. Magnolias everywhere? *I mean, really!* Even if it turns out *Architectural Digest* perfect, how do you hide a cat box, or do you take your cats to Dr. Kevorkian? Maybe we could drywall the cat box into its own little room. How do you say "cat box" in Spanish?

Now I want all the decorator touches—lamps, pictures, fancy curtain rods—and that (duh!) takes money. I suppose you could say it's a vicious circle, because wanting things makes you really love money, which I do right now.

God is a God of contentment. It's only when we get our eyes off of him and on our silly obsessions that we become discontent.

Dear Lord

Make me content in you. Help me care less about overkill with the magnolias and more about the fragrance of my life. May my contentment come from knowing you will never leave me or forsake me. Amen.

A NEW TAKE ON AN OLD STORY

When they saw the star, they were overjoyed.
On coming to the house, they saw the child
with his mother Mary, and they bowed
down and worshiped him.

MATTHEW 2:10–11

TRAFFIC SLOWED TO A snail's pace as Wayne and I made our way across town, hoping to get in a few more minutes of Christmas shopping before the stores closed. We were in our usual hurry mode and were more than slightly annoyed that it wasn't—and I'm not exactly proud of this, but it's true—caused by a wreck! You can make allowances for a wreck! In this case people were simply stopping traffic to rubber neck—inexcusable unless you're the one doing the looking, which is exactly what we were doing when it came our turn!

We couldn't believe our eyes. There were Mary, Joseph, and the baby (plastic figures lit from within) on a big ol' Harley Davidson Hawg covered in little twinkly lights. Joseph was in the driver's seat, Mary was hanging on for dear life, and the baby was on the handle bars. High above, jury-rigged to a light post, was the Christmas star twinkling down on this very bizarre scene.

The first word out of my mouth—and said in righteous indignation—was "sac-re-li-hi-gious!" Then we began to laugh, and we laughed till we almost wrecked the car. I'm embarrassed to say I drove by several more times that week, sometimes inviting friends to go along like it was some social event. Or maybe even a religious pilgrimage, for heaven's sake!

When you think about it, perhaps at another time in history the holy family *would* have traveled on a Harley. You'll have to admit the *original* Nativity scene was pretty unconventional, to say the least.

For the wise men, seeing the Christmas star over the house meant *they had found the right place*. The star was the evidence! No wonder they were overjoyed! Now they could offer their gifts! Now they could worship Christ the newborn King! The high point of their lifetime!

I wonder what happened when the excitement of the moment was over, after they paid their homage and started home. I wonder if they were as excited going back as they were on the way there. My guess is they weren't that different from you and me. They had their ups and downs. But were their lives changed? You'd better believe it! And I think what they discovered in retrospect was perhaps far more powerful than the event itself. I think they had a paradigm shift to end all paradigm shifts. They *became* the evidence—in a way they *became* the star—that would not only validate the event till the end of time, but would point the way to the Savior.

I want to be the evidence that points to the Savior. I guess you could say I wanna be a star!

Dear Lord

For the wise men, seeing the Christmas star meant they had found the right place. *No wonder they were overjoyed. Help me be overjoyed too when I see the Christmas star ... even a fake one jury-rigged to a light post. It points me to you. Amen.*

IF YOU'RE EUPHORIC, THINGS CAN'T BE ALL THAT BAD

There is a time for everything, and a season for every activity under heaven: a time to be born and a time to die, a time to plant and a time to uproot.

ECCLESIASTES 3:1–2

FIFTEEN YEARS AGO I had cancer and was told I might not live out the year. Of course that was bad news. The worst! But then I had this epiphany (No, e*pip*hany isn't the day we honor Gladys Knight's back-up singers, the Pips. It means "I had a revelation"!): Duh! If I'm going to die anyway, why not die happy? Why not indulge myself with chocolate to my heart's content?

With that in mind, I began to eat great quantities of milk chocolate. Just *milk* chocolate—the dark kind makes me jumpy. Every day of my life, for over sixteen years, I've eaten the equivalent of six to eight Hershey bars. I say "equivalent" because sometimes it's frozen Snickers Bars or a fudge binge.

Debbie, who owns the fudge shop at Farmer's Market, asks, "Having a lot of company again?" when she takes my money and hands me three pounds of fudge. *Well, noooo, not exactly.*

I'm no brain, but go figure! *Chocolate is the cure for cancer.* Why can I, with only a ninth-grade science class under my belt, understand this? Why some scientists—with degrees out the wazoo—can't see this is beyond me.

Don't scientists read newspapers? Are their eyeballs stuck to their microscopes? There have been several articles lately that would tell them—if they got their heads out of their petri dishes long enough to read them—that chocolate is a miracle "drug." A study was made using male graduates from an Ivy League university. It revealed that those who ate chocolate lived nearly a year longer than those who didn't; it's also known that chocolate releases endorphins into the system, causing a sense of euphoria, which, if nothing else, to my way of thinking, says, "If you're euphoric, things couldn't be all that bad." Duh, again!

The bottom line here is that regardless of modern science, God has a timetable for our lives. And for our deaths as well. I'll never forget the look on the doctor's face when he gave me what he believed were the facts based on his statistics. I'll never forget searching frantically for some piece of evidence that said I had a chance—that said I would live.

If I had died as the doctor predicted, I never would have witnessed Mindy's graduation from high school, or seen her in her prom dress, or taken pictures of her as homecoming princess. I would have missed Dana's graduation from college; missed seeing her fall head-over-heels for Barry. I would not have had the chance to help her plan her "Princess Diana" wedding, or help Wayne hang wallpaper in her new house. I never would have written a book—*I'm Alive and the Doctor's Dead,* which was the outgrowth of the journal I kept about having cancer, chemotherapy, and reconstructive surgery. And I never would have written my part of *Friends Through Thick and Thin,* or had a chance to meet all my wonderful new "old" friends because of the speaking engagements. I'm thankful that God is in charge, *not* the doctors!

Dear Lord

Don't let me become frantic when I hear the statistics. The computer doesn't know me—doesn't know how much I laugh and cry, how well I'm loved, who my friends are, or how I'm prayed for. It certainly doesn't know that you have a timetable for my life and that your timing is perfect. Amen.

CAN A HOG BE VACCINATED FOR CHICKEN POX?

Whatever you do, work at it with all your heart.

COLOSSIANS 3:23

WORK IS WORK, AND play is play. You can't get around it! As for me, I'd rather play, so sometimes I turn my work into play to fool myself. The problem is, if your work looks like play your friends are bound to say, "That woman doesn't do a lick of work; all she does is have fun!" Tenacity and "working with all your heart" do pay off, however, and I can give you a perfect example. You'll have to make up your own mind. Was it work or was it play?

It happened over thirty years ago soon after we moved to Nashville. Halloween was just around the corner, and it was time to buy a pumpkin—a big, fat, orange pumpkin. We liked the kind that were so big Wayne had to use his electric drill to carve faces on them.

Much to our surprise, there wasn't a big orange pumpkin to be found—at least not the kind we were used to. All we could find were these pinkish, pale-looking, misshapen, gourd-like things.

When I complained to my neighbor Alice (whose daughter Mary was my Mindy's best friend), she agreed. "I've never been able to find pumpkins in Tennessee like we were used to in Indiana," she said. "We should drive up there and get some."

"Let's get a whole truckload and set up a pumpkin stand," I joked. "There certainly seems to be a market for them!"

The more we talked the more excited we became—and the more our husbands freaked out! At one point my husband asked, "Is it the money? How much do you want?" and offered to give me whatever profit I thought I might make if only I'd quit talking about it.

Alice's husband, Joe, didn't say much, but it was obvious neither he nor Wayne wanted their wives sitting by the side of the road selling pumpkins! And being astute businessmen, they were eager to point out there wasn't a chance in a million we'd make any money. In fact, they were sure we'd lose our shirts (make that blouses!).

Not easily dissuaded, we searched for and found a twenty-four hour gas station that had a big grassy triangle on the corner of a busy intersection; it was perfect for our new business. When we approached the owner and asked how much he would charge, he looked at us like we were from Mars and had just asked him to check the transmission in our space ship!

He stood on one foot, then the other, pulled his George Dickel Tennessee Whiskey ball cap off, and scratched his head with his greasy hand. You could tell his wheels were turning. "Well, I never!" he said and thought some more. We never had either, but we weren't about to admit it! He was obviously trying to kill time. He pulled out his big red bandanna, shifted his cud of chewing tobacco to the other cheek, wiped his brow like he'd just done a major engine overhaul, and broke out in a smile.

"Lawrd, ladies. G'wan and take it. You don't have to pay me nothin'. You ain't gonna make nothin' anyway."

That taken care of, all we had to do was find pumpkins somewhere out there in the "great beyond" and get them to Nashville. We began making phone calls to everyone we knew in Indiana, Ohio, and Illinois. We could find pumpkins but couldn't find a way to get them to Nashville.

Several times we had our deal lined up, but then it would fall apart at the last minute. The best possibility at one point was my farmer-relatives in Ohio who, as luck would have it, happened to have a truck dead-heading to Tennessee to pick up hogs at exactly the right time. It would be no problem at all to send a load of pumpkins. We were ecstatic! Then, would you believe, there was a swine quarantine—mumps or chicken pox I suppose—and the hogs couldn't travel. No hogs, no pumpkins! We were brokenhearted.

When my husband left for California on a business trip, our plans had gone down the tubes for the umpteenth time. The last thing he said before he got on the plane was, "I hope I never hear another word about pumpkins!" Then he added, "By the way, there's a man coming this afternoon to deliver firewood."

When the truck—the nicest long flatbed truck you've ever seen—pulled up that afternoon and the man began to unload wood, a light bulb went on over my head. "Nice truck," I said. "Ever haul anything besides wood?"

"Yeh—do."

"Like for instance could you haul … oh, what? I don't know. Let's see … just pick something out of the air. Pumpkins—that's it! Could you haul pumpkins?"

"Yeh—could."

"Do people ever pay you to go out of town? Out of state? Like pick a place. Say Indiana—go to Indiana and back?"

"Yeh—th' do."

"Interesting," I said as I hurried inside to call Alice.

Before I had a chance to pick up the phone, it rang. It was my father-in-law in Indiana. "Honey, I've found pumpkins for you." (Heaven help! Wayne's own father, part of the enemy camp. Who would have thought!) "Any idea how we could get them to Nashville?"

Before we knew it, we had pumpkins—six tons of perfect bright orange pumpkins—we were in business! Before the first day was over, we'd been visited by the newspapers, television stations, and we'd made the news service! Our picture was on the front page of newspapers all over the country (my brother-in-law had a news clipping service and sent me all of them). And Wayne was on his way home from California without a clue!

Never let it be said, though, that Wayne and Joe didn't get on the bandwagon. At first they drove by slowly and glanced our way. Then they parked at the back of the lot and observed from a distance. It wasn't long, however, before you'd have thought it was *their* idea.

We had a ball! We didn't just sell pumpkins, we drew faces, put hats and earrings on them, and gave them names. We even handed out recipes. Our friends got involved; they brought casseroles and picnics for dinner each night and couldn't tear themselves away. They stayed for the evening.

We met new friends. One man drove across town to buy a pumpkin, having heard about us on the radio. He gave me his card. "I'm a lawyer, just starting out," he said, "and you seem like the kind of person who could get in trouble easily and might need a lawyer to get you out of jail." He was joking; his card said he was a *corporate lawyer*. Duh! Even I know a corporate lawyer doesn't bail you out of jail!

We ran out of pumpkins long before Halloween, but we didn't care; we'd made a *bundle!* Joyfully, I spent my share on the biggest, cushiest lounge chair I could find. A gift for my husband!

Wayne and I had been contemplating starting a new company and hadn't quite had the guts to do it. Somehow this small success pushed us over the edge and we decided to call a lawyer. "Know any?" he asked. I handed him the card from my pumpkin purchaser. Wayne made the call and said how he happened to have the man's name and number. When he went into an explanation as to why he was calling, the young lawyer interrupted him: "I understand who you are! You want a divorce, right?"

We went on to form a strong relationship with the lawyer, and he helped Wayne set up the business. Perhaps it never would have happened had we not had a successful pumpkin stand.

God's family is made up of all sorts of "worker bees." Some make work look like play—the ones who are always front and center. They sing, play instruments, perform drama, preach, and teach. Then there are those whose work *really looks like work!* They dish soup to the poor, tutor kids in the inner city, build homes for the less fortunate, work in church kitchens, or do the janitor work at church.

Whatever the job is that God has called you and me to do, he wants us to go at it like there's no tomorrow—with all our hearts! "And whatever you do, whether in word or deed, do it all in the name of the Lord Jesus, giving thanks to God the Father through him" (Colossians 3:17).

Dear Lord

Whatever I do, let me do it with all my heart. And thank you for those who are front and center, who are leaders (the job comes with huge responsibility); let the rest of us be encouragers. And I pray a special blessing on those who are behind the scenes, often in thankless jobs. Help us all remember to say "thank you." I'm especially grateful, Lord, for those who have given me the gift of their enthusiasm—those who have said, "You can do it," or "You did a good job." May I be a cheerleader, an encourager, and may I be tenacious when it comes to doing your work. Amen.

THE THREE BEARS GO TO CAMELOT

I will lie down and sleep in peace, for you
alone, O LORD, make me dwell in safety.

PSALM 4:8

SLEEPING IS NOT USUALLY a problem for me. Once in awhile I traipse through the house half the night, or flip the remote control till my thumb is numb, or sit on the sun deck and listen to night sounds, or even sit *inside* and listen to night sounds—Wayne snoring!

Wayne has always snored. Years ago he traveled to Alaska with two other men. The accommodations were such that they had to sleep in the same room. Each night Wayne would be the first to doze off, and much to the consternation of the others, he would immediately begin to saw logs. One night in sheer frustration one of the men got out his trusty tape recorder and proceeded to "interview" Wayne.

"We are here in Alaska travelling with the world-famous adventurer-photographer, Wayne Buchanan. Wayne, I understand you've been all over the world. You must lead a very exciting life. Could you comment on that?"

"Snore! Snore!"

"Tell us, Wayne, how did you feel today when we were flying between mountain peaks and ice formed on the plane's wings and we began to lose altitude?"

"Snore! Snore! Snore!"

And on and on! Naturally the tape was prized by Wayne's travelling companions and was played at many parties.

Our friend Bob MacKenzie also is a very sound sleeper. More than once he's been on a plane and slept right through his destination. Once he arrived in Los Angeles, and without telling them he was coming, showed up at the home of our mutual friends, Lois and Fred Bock. Seeing they had dinner guests, he simply went through the backyard, into the guest house and went to bed.

Sometime during the evening Fred was asked about the little house at the back of the property. When told it was Fred's studio and also a guest house, one of the men, himself a musician, asked for a tour.

In a story that would remind you for all the world of *The Three Bears*, there, to their surprise was Bob, sleeping like a baby. They called his name. No response. After several tries, Fred tiptoed to the piano, and with a flourish, began the introduction to "If Ever I Would Leave You."

The guest just happened to be a great actor known best for his role in *Camelot*. He took his cue, assumed his Camelot-like stance, and began to sing his signature song at the top of his lungs. Still no response. Bob slept on. When the last note was sung they turned out the light and left.

It's comforting to know that we can lie down and sleep in peace. For a long time after I had cancer I woke up in terror, sure that the disease was hiding someplace in my body ready to strike me dead at any moment. Later, there were times I worried about one of my daughters and never fully relaxed and slept. Sometimes now when I watch the news just before bedtime, I'm uneasy because of the horrible stories I see and hear. Then I remind myself of God's care, that I can throw myself into his arms with total abandonment, trusting fully.

Dear Lord

"I will lie down and sleep in peace." Apparently Wayne has a good grasp of that Scripture. Bob, too! I pray that for myself, not because the wakefulness is so annoying (and it is!), but because I will experience the peace of resting in the safety of your arms. Amen.

OF MICE AND (JUST THE) MEN-TION OF TRAPS

Everyone has to die once, then face the consequences.

HEBREWS 9:27 (THE MESSAGE)

PEGGY KNOWS EXACTLY WHAT to do if I should die suddenly. She has her orders! Before my body is cold, she's supposed to nose around, see that I've left this earth in an orderly fashion, and take care of anything that might be left undone.

For instance, I'd want her to make sure there's nothing disgusting growing in my refrigerator, like rotten lettuce or moldy cheese, unless by chance I'm in the middle of an experiment like maybe growing my own penicillin.

Peggy would know instinctively that I wouldn't want a dirty cup or glass in the sink, and she'd know to slice a lemon and run it through the disposal to give it a fresh smell. If they should carry me out feet first and the bed wasn't made, she would make it.

I'd want her to look around for anything that might embarrass me, like the dirt under the big kitchen rug. When I cook I kick crumbs and crud under it to be dealt with at a later time. Often a *much* later time! She knows about the mouse traps in the bread drawer and would know to remove them so as not to encourage those gossipy types who would say, "Long before she died, she'd gone a little batty. I've heard she had you-know-whats in her you-know-where. If that's not crazy, I don't know what is."

There's a perfectly logical explanation for the you-know-whats in the you-know-where! Several years ago we discovered telltale traces of mice in our bread drawer. We spoke to our two cats about it and they assured us (mostly by their blank looks) that had these sneaky little rodents set foot in *their* kitchen, they would have known about it and acted immediately, if not sooner. From that we concluded the mice had "broken and entered" through the back of the bread drawer.

With an "I'll fix them," I headed straight to the hardware store, bought traps, and put them in the bread drawer. I intended to go back later and set them. (Would you leave your mouse-traps sitting out in plain sight? I don't think so.) Perhaps just the sight of the traps scared the mice back into the woods. I never set the traps and never saw mouse mess again.

Thank heavens for Peggy. She would fix things and I could rest in peace, knowing I'd covered all my bases here on earth. Having my bases covered for the hereafter is quite another thing! I'm thankful that God didn't have to make arrangements as elaborate as mine when he planned for our eternal destiny. He only asked us to accept that his Son Jesus paid the consequences for our sin and to live our lives in gratitude and obedience. What could be simpler?

Dear Lord

You must laugh when you see the silly things that cause me to be obsessed. Help me live in light of the eternal ... because after that ... Eeek! There will be consequences! But then again, there will be rewards too. Let me live with that in mind. Amen.

SHE THOUGHT THE GREAT DEPRESSION WAS HER MARRIAGE!

Celebrate God all day, every day. I mean,
revel in him! Make it as clear as you can to
all you meet that you're on their side, work-
ing with them and not against them.

PHILIPPIANS 4:4 (THE MESSAGE)

IN MY FILE FOLDER marked "stuff that's just too good to throw away" is a postcard with the well-known picture of the sour-faced pitchfork-holding farmer and his equally sour-faced (and ugly to boot) wife. The tag line is: "Don't speak to them, Harold, they don't go to our church." These old characters obviously didn't celebrate God all day, every day, much less revel in him! We may not look quite that bad, but you'll have to admit very few of us "celebrate God all day, every day" as the Scripture implies we should.

We used to have a neighbor whose outlook on life was less than rosy; her proverbial cup was always half empty. It hadn't been *her day* for as long as we could remember, and she wouldn't recognize a joke if it was lit up in neon.

She griped about her kids, and she griped about her husband (her wedding band was a mood ring). We longed to tell her about Prozac.

On what seemed to be the most perfect day of the year, several of us gathered for a cup of coffee. We were sitting outside on the patio, literally ooh-ing and ah-ing over the beauty of the early spring morning.

"This day just makes me mad," she announced for all to hear. You could hear a pin drop. We were baffled. "Why in the world does it make you mad?" we asked. "'Cause I know it's not going to last."

Since that time Wayne and I have often repeated those words. We'll roll over in bed, see the sun is shining, and one of us will say, "This day just makes me mad."

Actually, I could celebrate God all day, every day, if it weren't for other people! It's just that they keep doing things that hinder my celebration. Like cutting me off on the expressway. Or putting the wrong thing in my McDonald's bag (pancakes instead of Big Breakfast).

It's always other people! Not getting back to me with the information I need to finish *their* project. Or getting back to me with the *wrong information* and expecting me to figure it out. Or calling me—on *my* phone, for heaven's sake—to sell me *their* cemetery plots, or their newspapers, or THEIR STUPID LONG DISTANCE SERVICES! PHEW! THIS DAY IS ALREADY STARTING TO MAKE ME MAD!

As for showing all those you meet that you're on their side, working with them and not against them, *puh-leeze!* Get a life! This is not possible. How can you do that when you so totally disagree with what they are doing? Sometimes they are doing it in God's name, for heaven's sake!

I don't judge people unless I have to, BUT . . . ! *Those* Pentecostals couldn't be one bit pleasing to the Lord the way they get so carried away. They practically *hang from the chandeliers!* The Independents are worse! They spend all their time judging the Pentecostals—too self-righteous for their own good. And

Catholics? Don't you know about them? All those fancy churches! What a waste! Don't even get me started on the Baptists; and if you ask me (or even if you don't), the Methodists are hopelessly off the track, practically New Age. And the Presbyterians have all—*I'm talkin' all*—gone liberal! *Wait! Not all of us, I'm a Presbyterian!*

I'm joking! Duh! Do I have to tell you? I'm trying to make a point—celebrating God all day, every day is a real challenge! It's a challenge, but it's doable. Maybe not all at once, but maybe we can start small and sneak up on it! Maybe try it once a week, then twice a week, then once a day (say, all morning) and finally *all day, every day*. I'll try if you will!

With a little fear and trepidation (No, I don't agree with every word; and yes, I think there are some wrong theologies mixed in), but in the hope of a better understanding, I submit to you a portion of a litany that has helped me be less judgmental of others. It was written by the students and staff at Appalachian Ministries Educational Resource Center. AMERC calls itself "a consortium of theological institutions and denominations that offers graduate-level training to seminarians, clergy and lay leaders for ministry in small town and rural churches." They don't teach theology, they teach the students how to work with people. If your beliefs differ from some of the denominations listed here, I ask you to move beyond that and adopt the spirit that is intended.

> *Let us give thanks for the churches which form Christ's worldwide Church. There is one Body and one Spirit, one Lord, one faith, one baptism.*
>
> *We thank You for the churches named after Your servant, Martin Luther: For their witness to the primacy of Your Word and of Your gift of faith, by which alone, we are justified.*
>
> *We glorify You, O God, for the churches of the Reformed family: For their stress upon Your sovereignty and our responsibility within Your covenant.*

We praise You for the churches of the Baptist tradition: For their insistence upon the freedom of Your Holy Spirit and our need to be born again by that Spirit.

We thank You for the churches of the African-American tradition: For their determination to see Christ's gospel fleshed out in all of our society.

We glorify You for the United Church of Christ: For their vigorous defense of independence and their emphasis on local initiative.

We are grateful, O God, for the Roman Catholic Church: For the stirring of her worship, her grand system of law, her vocations for body living.

We are grateful, O God, for the churches of Methodism: For their testimony to Your demand for a disciplined Christian life and for social justice.

We praise You for Your people known as Friends: For the simple dignity of their meetings, their respect for the inner light, and their commitment to non-violence.

We are grateful, O God, for the Church of the Nazarene: For their commitment to the direct work of the Holy Spirit and sanctification of the believer.

We thank You for the Christian Church (Disciples of Christ): For showing us all how to hold together deep conviction, vigorous action, and winsome spirit.

We thank You for the manifold community of Evangelical and Pentecostal churches: For the joyous abandon of their worship, their sacrificial stewardship, their evangelistic fervor.

We thank You for the union and community churches: For their dedication to making one witness.

O God, Whose divine Son prayed that we might all be one: Accept our thanksgiving for the diversity which marks the life of His Church, but remind us evermore, there is one Body and one Spirit, one Lord, one faith, one baptism. Amen.

Dear Lord

Even though it's the other person who is really the problem, help me be responsible for me. Maybe they'll catch on. I want to celebrate you. Revel in you. Help me. Amen.

WHEN I GET ONE MORE HOLE PUNCHED IN MY CARD, I'LL GET A FREEBIE AT HOUSE OF TATTOOS

*Therefore, I urge you, brothers, in view of
God's mercy, to offer your bodies as living
sacrifices, holy and pleasing to God—this is
your spiritual act of worship.*

ROMANS 12:1

SOMETIMES WHEN I SPEAK, I tell my audience I'm from West Virginia. "But I'll have you know, I wear shoes," I say. They laugh. "And," I continue, "my tattoos are spelled correctly." I used to get a huge response to that; people fell on the floor laughing. Lately people barely chuckle and I finally figured out it's because nowadays so many people really do have tattoos— maybe more people than we know, since tattoos can be easily hidden under their clothing. Should some foreign dictator move in to take over the government, strip-search us, and line us up naked, we might be surprised out of our minds. We might even find out the preacher has one!

I spoke in a southern city not long ago, and afterward a young woman told me her husband was a "Christian tattoo artist." I'm sure I looked shocked—I have to admit I was picturing the Last

Supper on someone's hip—but her explanation made sense. "He was a regular tattoo artist and then he found God. Now he just does religious art like angels, and hearts, and Scripture," she said. "Also, removing tattoos is painful and costly—it has to be done little by little and can take months or even years—so he keeps busy just covering obscene words and putting clothes on naked bodies." Who am I to say this is not a ministry?

I had a tattoo once, if only for an evening. Wayne and I were invited to a Sunday school party where everyone was supposed to dress "tacky." Now that's right up my alley!

The same couldn't be said for Wayne. He managed to rummage around, however, and found a leather jacket, stuck a cigarette between his lips, and struck a James Dean pose—albeit a rather chunky James Dean.

I stood on my head in the box of old clothes I keep for such occasions, and came up with a shiny, brown, Cher-type, polyester outfit with bell-bottom pants and lots of ostrich feathers around the sleeves and hem. The neckline was slightly scandalous for a Sunday school party; but my thoughts were, "If they want tacky, I'll give them tacky."

Wow! Was I stunning—spelled s-l-e-a-z-y!

"More is better," I said as I added heavy blue eye shadow. Then came an inspiration. "A tattoo. I need a tattoo," I squealed as I pulled my blouse off one shoulder and picked up my eyebrow pencil. Wayne rolled his eyes.

"Wayne" I scrawled on my chest, drew a heart around it, and pulled my top back in place. As for positioning, it couldn't have been better if I had planned it. "AYNE" it read, the W disappearing into the mysterious unknown of the cleavage. Talk about effect!

It was fun to see what our friends considered tacky: a golf outfit with high-heeled evening shoes, a strapless evening gown with a tee shirt under it, a necktie with an undershirt. Six men showed up like self-fulfilling prophecies—Bermuda shorts and tee shirts with black dress shoes and socks. I'm happy to say, there

was only one James Dean and not another soul with a tattoo that
said "AYNE." I mean, "WAYNE."

The verse in Romans about offering our bodies holy and
pleasing to God is followed by a verse that smacks you in the
face. It tells you to be "transformed by the renewing of your
mind," and transformed means "changed in form, nature, or
character." The unabridged dictionary even says "to change into
another substance." Eeeek! That's like *transmutation*—like in a science fiction movie—like changing from one species to another!
Like becoming new creatures in Christ, for heaven's sake! In that
new state, "Then you will be able to test and approve what
God's will is—his good, pleasing, and perfect will."

Ooooo! I don't want to be judgmental, but doesn't this all
sound too . . . what? A little too weird? Too science fiction-ish?
Too New Ageish?

I'm joking! God is dead serious, though, about how he can
and does change us!

Dear Lord

*This is amazing stuff! That I could be changed from one species
to another by the renewing of my mind. A new creature in
Christ! I pray for this and I offer my body as your temple, a living sacrifice, holy, acceptable, and pleasing to you. Amen.*

PARDON ME, SIR, BUT THERE'S ICING ON THE SEAT OF YOUR PANTS

*For I am the least of the apostles and do not
even deserve to be called an apostle ... But
by the grace of God I am what I am, and
his grace to me was not without effect.*

1 CORINTHIANS 15: 9–10

NOT LONG AGO AT a conference I attended in California, one of the speakers (a Christian author) seemed to me to be rather arrogant. Not only that, but (again, in my not-so-humble opinion) he sprinkled his talk with little innuendos of male superiority. Specifically his *own* male superiority. At one point he referred to his wife in a demeaning manner. It was nothing blatant; had it been blatant you could've gone up to him afterward, stuck your fingernail up his nose, twisted it, and confronted! He was ever so subtle.

That night the group took a cruise around San Francisco Bay, and during dinner and the ensuing table-talk, I found I wasn't the only one who felt the speaker came off as both arrogant and chauvinistic. Men and women alike agreed. About that time, we noticed that our speaker friend was making his way to the buffet table, honing in on the desserts.

With an "I'll fix him," one of the women jumped up and made a beeline for a three-tiered chocolate cake with raspberry filling and gooey white frosting. After turning to make sure she had an audience (she did!), she—in one continuous motion—grabbed a plate and fork and dumped a big piece of cake on the plate. Then she loaded the fork with cake—heavy on frosting—and positioned herself behind Mr. You-Know-Who.

The self-appointed actress played her audience well. They were really into it, cheering her on, when suddenly a put-on-the-brakes kind of expression came across her face. Just as she had her fork poised in the vicinity of our speaker-friend's derrière, ready to splatter frosting across the seat of his pants, a waiter—who appeared out of nowhere—stepped in, firmly took hold of her wrist and said loudly and dramatically, "Oh, my dear, puh-leeze let me take that for you."

He then turned to us—we applauded—and took his bow, proud that he'd not only upstaged the star by a mile, but he'd saved the day as well. Next he gave the "actress" a push toward her chair and bent over our table. He opened his mouth to say something, but changed his mind. Instead he shook his head, made a "Tsk! Tsk!" sound with his tongue, wagged his finger, and gave us a look that said he'd call the cake patrol if we gave him another minute's trouble.

I'll have to admit it occurred to me that the man in question, our morning speaker, didn't *deserve* to be "an apostle." Well, maybe he deserved to be one, but certainly not one who stands in front of others as a leader—*as an example*, for heaven's sake! But wait! What about me? I don't deserve to be an apostle either, *certainly not an apostle who stands in front of others as a leader—as an example,* for heaven's sake! But wait again! I forgot about *grace,* God's unmerited favor, which means letting me off the hook even though I don't deserve it. It's his grace that makes all the difference in my life, in my effectiveness; and now that I think of it, it should make a difference in my behavior!

Note: If you think the actress in this story was funny, or even somewhat amusing, it was I. But if you think the actress in this story was disgusting and judgmental, it was obviously some obnoxious woman from New York City.

For your grace I'm on-my-face thankful. Humbled beyond words. Without it my actions are just that, my *actions. They are selfish and arrogant and ineffective. Often they are degrading to other people. I want to be effective for you. Teach me how to show grace to others using your example. Amen.*

AN ELECTRIC BLANKET FOR A STREET PERSON?

For he will deliver the needy who cry out,
the afflicted who have no one to help.

PSALM 72:12

A FRIEND OF MINE who lives in San Francisco insists someday she'll be a street person. This lady has a high-paying job, lives in an expensive apartment, and is accustomed to the finer things in life. However, if you should meet up with her, you'll find that instead of a leather briefcase she carries a paper shopping bag, a reminder, she says, that if ever she has to choose between living in a nursing home or living on the streets, she'd choose the streets.

She carries her shopping bag everywhere, including to her high-powered business meetings; when she describes her future street-person life, she makes it sound rather intriguing and says she'll have no responsibility except to her two cat companions. She makes the comparison to being propped up in a nursing home and being fed through tubes; believe me, it's almost convincing, until you walk out into the streets of San Francisco and reality hits you.

Near my office in Nashville lives a whole community of street people who have taken up residence under the interstate highway bridge. One young man touches me deeply. He's probably mentally ill. His eyes say "nobody's home." Perhaps his brain is hopelessly altered from drug abuse.

We know of one person who lived on the streets and yet whose family lives in a big roomy house close by with warm beds fat with down comforters, a friendly fireplace, and a refrigerator packed with delicious and nourishing food. Not only would they have welcomed her but would have loved to lavish her with all the things she so desperately needed.

My husband, too, has been touched by the increasing number of people who stand for hours at a time with signs that say "I will work for food." On occasion, he's even taken some of them shopping. But usually his efforts are rejected, because what they really want is money.

Jan and Ed, friends of long standing, are very proactive in helping these needy souls in a tangible way. After watching a street person for several weeks, Jan took the down comforter from her bed and gave it to Ed with instructions to "deliver it to the man who lives under a semi-trailer in Green Hills." Ed swears it was an electric blanket, and we tease Jan unmercifully about giving an electric blanket to someone who has no home, much less electricity.

One night Ed stopped to chat with his new friend. It was freezing cold and his teeth were chattering. "Tell you what," Ed said. "Let's walk over there to that fried chicken restaurant and I'll buy us some hot coffee and dinner."

"Are you kidding?" answered the homeless man. "I can't eat that greasy stuff."

That story makes us laugh, but I'm thinking it's not unlike how we treat our heavenly Father. He offers us everything, and we accept so little. We settle for the streets. Cardboard boxes to sleep in and garbage to eat! And loneliness! He wants to lavish us with more than we can ever fathom. He has a full refrigerator and warm beds with down comforters and loving arms to hold us. All we need to do is accept what he offers.

Dear Lord

Let me be aware of those who need my help. Let my eyes be open and help me care. Help me act! And, Father, don't let me settle for living on the streets spiritually because of my own stupid self-sufficiency. May I graciously accept your lavish provisions. May I live in your riches! Amen.

WHEN I THINK ABOUT HEAVEN, I THINK ABOUT ALL THE FANCY STUFF!

The twelve gates were twelve pearls, each gate made of a single pearl. The great street of the city was of pure gold, like transparent glass.

REVELATION 21:21

MOST PEOPLE I KNOW say they couldn't care less about all the fancy stuff heaven has to offer, they just want to be with the Lord. Not me! Wait! *I don't mean I don't want to be with the Lord,* I just mean I really like the idea of all that fancy stuff, too!

Ever since I was a little bitty girl, I've liked the fancy stuff. Everyone who knows me knows that I've never gotten over being Mrs. Vandertweezers, the name I gave myself as a child when I would dress up in fancy clothes and walk around the neighborhood with my cat, Smokey the Pirate Don Derk of Don Day. In my book *I'm Alive and the Doctor's Dead* I describe Mrs. Vandertweezers to a T, and I can assure you *she* liked the fancy stuff!

I've heard ministers preach whole sermons on the fact that our minds can't begin to comprehend how magnificent heaven will be, that our mortal minds just can't handle it. Well, I don't want to brag, but mine can! I can just picture me wearing my big ol' crown.

If you've ever watched Miss America, you know it's not easy walking with a crown on your head. I've already practiced my crown-wearing. I have a gold plastic one, with fake jewels, that I bought when my nieces, Cara and Kirby, were little girls. I would put it on and say, "I'm the queen of everything, and you *will* do exactly as I say." Even though now they are teenagers, I still do my act and they pretend to enjoy it. (Perhaps *tolerate* is a better word!)

I can picture those gates made from humongous pearls, and streets so bright you have to put on your movie-star-sized sunglasses before you take a walk. I can see myself walking up and down those streets of gold talking to all my friends—the very same friends who said they didn't care about all the fancy stuff when they were on earth, but are really *getting into it* now that they are in heaven.

Heaven is a real place. A place to look forward to, to contemplate. To prepare for. As the song says, "Wait Till You See Me in My New Home!"

Dear God

Thank you that life's not over when we die, that you have prepared this incredible place to look forward to. I want to be ready. I want to be right with you. Let me show the way to others by the way I live. I, for one, am glad heaven is full of all that fancy stuff. Don't hold back! Amen.

YOU DON'T HAVE TO BE A THEOLOGIAN TO "GET IT"

Jesus declared, "I tell you the truth, no one can see the kingdom of God unless he is born again."

JOHN 3:3

IN JOHN 3:3 JESUS is answering Nicodemus, who has a once-in-a-lifetime opportunity to play "twenty questions"—*in person*—with the Savior, and still doesn't get it!

Even today, a lot of people don't get it. They get really hung up on the "B.A." phrase. I'm no theologian (surprise, surprise!), but for me what being "born again" boils down to is "accepting God's perspective and living by it." It means spiritually "getting it."

And duh! According to the verse, if you don't "get it" you won't go to heaven; because, unless I'm way off base, "kingdom of God" means heaven!

My friend Hal Ezell was Western Region Commissioner of Immigration for the U.S. and coauthor of Proposition 187, which was designed to stop the flow of illegal immigrants into the United States. Hal wasn't opposed to immigration; he was opposed to *illegal* immigration. At his memorial service there were thirty or more immigrants who stood to honor him for personally helping them become citizens of our country. One man praised him for not only helping him become a citizen, but for paying to furnish his apartment as well.

One of the eulogizers at Hal's funeral joked that when Hal walked up to heaven's gates, "with his cocky, assured kind of swagger," St. Peter stopped him. "Wait here," he said. "I have to check to see if it's legal for you to get into this place." After a long wait, the gates are opened and St. Peter says, "Come on in," to which Hal replies, "Thank God I'm finally in a place where there are no illegals."

Hal wanted it done the right way. And duh, again! *God* also wants it done the right way. Matter of fact, he demands it! He isn't going to allow it to be done *any other* way.

Some people think if they live a good life but without a relationship with God and keep their noses clean they'll be welcomed into heaven like a long lost cousin. Others believe they are so rotten to the core they are beyond help. "Oh, I'll just go to hell; all my friends will be there anyway." Both theories are wrong. God wants an intimate relationship with us, and, no matter what we have done, we are equally needy in his sight. He wants us to ask for forgiveness and to know him *personally*.

Dear God

I pray for my friends who don't live in your perspective. I pray that they'll "get it," that they will choose the right way so that when "St. Peter checks the list," they'll be on it. Amen.

PECAN PIE WITH HORSERADISH? IT'S A SOUTHERN THING

*I will sing of the LORD's great love forever;
with my mouth I will make your faithfulness
known through all generations.*

PSALM 89:1

WHEN WE FIRST MOVED to Nashville from a suburb near Chicago, we sometimes felt we were intruders into a culture that had things pretty much the way they liked it and wanted to keep it that way. They didn't need any know-it-all *Yankee* sticking even a single toe into their sacred territory. We learned fast: "y'all" is singular; "all y'all" is plural; "all y'all's" is plural possessive; and if it can't be fried in bacon grease, it ain't worth cookin'. Little did I know that an iron skillet would open the door wide enough for me to stick my whole foot in.

One night early on, we had a little dinner party, and during the course of the evening one of the women noticed our iron skillet.

"Well loo-wok [at the time I didn't know that "look" was a two-syllable word and that it had a w in it] evreh-body," said my guest. "Go in thay-ah and loo-wok. The Buchanans have an ah-ron skeelit. They couldn't be all bay-ad if they have an ah-ron skeelit."

I explained that I use an iron skillet because my mother (who was from *southern* Ohio) used one, and that my grand-mothers on both sides of my family (also from *southern* Ohio) used them. I said mine was a gift from my mother-in-law (*south-ern* Indiana!) who gave it to me with such reverence you would have thought it was a silver teapot. These steel magnolias under-stood the generational thing about skillets. In fact, they saw me in a new light—almost (but not quite!) like I was one of them!

I've found there's a generational thing about recipes too, and these southern belles intend to keep it that way. Translated (at least in this case) the word "generational" must mean "within the generations of *my own family and nobody else's*." Should you ask, they're too nice to turn you down, so they'll give you a recipe that is very much like the original with the exception of two or three added mystery ingredients.

"Ah'd be gla-ad to give you mah recipe fo-wah mah pe-can ['can' as in *can of tuna fish*] pah. How nahce of you to ask," she'll say. "Wah, it's been in mah family fo-wah ev-ah, passed down from gen-ah-ration to gen-ah-ration."

She'll look you right in the eye and smile the *sah-weet-est* smile you can imagine when she hands it over. It seems I'm not the only northern transplant to receive a recipe for pecan pie that calls for a *half cup of horseradish and a tablespoon of red pepper!*

There must be a hundred verses of Scripture with the word "generation" or "generations" in them. That word should be a reminder each time we see it, that the continuity of family and the principles it embraces are important for the kingdom. We have a huge responsibility to pass our faith on to our children and grandchildren and teach them to do likewise. We pass on our traditions (including our panache for entertaining!) and heir-looms, skillets and recipes, not to mention our bad habits. How much more important it is to pass on our faith.

Dear Lord

You are forever and ever: I promise to make your faithfulness known to the next generation, just as my parents and grandparents did. I pray that my daughters will accept that responsibility too. Amen.

TWO SHALL BE AS ONE; THEN AGAIN, MAYBE NOT!

> *Observe the Sabbath day by keeping it holy,*
> *as the LORD your God has commanded you.*
>
> DEUTERONOMY 5:12

WHEN I WAS A child, people didn't work on Sunday regardless of their religious affiliation. Those who didn't go to church still rested on Sunday, if for no other reason, maybe out of respect for those who did. Seldom did you hear a lawn mower on the "Lord's Day." Stores were closed, even grocery stores; and if you traveled on Sunday, it was almost impossible to find a service station open, much less a restaurant.

There was a law in those days called the *blue law*. It actually prohibited businesses from opening on Sunday. I can't for the life of me think why the law would be called "blue." Maybe the guy who thought it up didn't like his wife and it made him blue to have to stay home with her all day. Perhaps his shirt was too tight and his face turned blue. Maybe the law was written on blue paper. I don't know.

Mother wouldn't even let me sew doll clothes on Sunday. "Every stitch you sew on Sunday, you'll have to take it out with your nose on Monday," she said. In all these years, I've yet to find that verse in the Bible.

My mother-in-law, a minister's wife, was even more adamant about keeping the Sabbath, although I never saw her work harder than when she was preparing for and cleaning up after Sunday dinner.

When I was pregnant with Dana, I wanted to use Mom Buchanan's sewing machine to make my maternity clothes. At the time I was working forty hours a week and commuting two hours a day to and from my job; Saturdays had a tendency to get away from me. The only day left seemed to be Sunday, but I never dared ask, knowing Mom's opinion on that subject. One Sunday, however, Mom and Dad went out of town and I decided to seize the opportunity.

It's important to note that when Mom's sewing machine—an ancient treadle number—wasn't in use, it was covered with a clean starched dish towel with big red cherries all over it.

Since I can barely walk and chew gum at the same time, making this fine machine work was a monumental task. You had to put both your feet on the treadle and pump it back and forth like you were possessed with some sort of St. Vitus' dance. At the same time, with both hands, you had to guide the material under the presser foot. I never *ever* got the hang of it!

Fortunately for me, Wayne—always ready to meet a challenge, even sometimes when there is no challenge to meet—devised a system. As I guided the fabric under the presser foot, he would lie on the floor on his stomach and operate the treadle with his hands. Picture it if you will!

I can't honestly say that Wayne and I "worked as one" that Sunday, but somehow we managed to finish two outfits and get the mess cleaned up before his folks returned. Barely! I was frantically stuffing the clothes and the leftover fabric into a paper bag, and Wayne was crawling around picking up thread from the carpet, as they drove into the driveway.

The next day, when I pulled one of the dresses over my head to try it on, there—sewn right down the center seam—was Mom's cherry-covered dish towel, just flappin' in the wind!

Funny, I'll sometimes grocery shop on Sunday or weed my flower garden, but you'll never ever catch me sewing. No sir-ee, not this girl. I guess you could say it's a nose thing.

Here's a tough one! *Today is Sunday and tomorrow I have a full day. We've just recovered from an ice storm and I'm out of groceries. And then there's the dress at McClure's I've been thinking about; it's probably on sale by now, and it'll be gone if I wait. While I'm out I could pick up that zipper I need at Hancock, and that's in the same neighborhood as Wal-Mart. I don't really need anything at Wal-Mart, but I'm sure once I get there I'll fill a basket.*

Or I could observe the Sabbath and keep it holy as my parents taught me to do, and God's Word teaches me to do.

Dear Lord

I've not done too well with this Sabbath thing. Help me honor your instructions and the memory of my parents. Amen.

WE THOUGHT THEY WERE ASLEEP TILL THEY SAID AMEN

Jesus said, "Let the little children come to me, and do not hinder them, for the kingdom of heaven belongs to such as these."

MATTHEW 19:14

IT'S FUNNY THAT JESUS tells his disciples not to hinder the little children in their pursuit of him. He certainly must have thought children were able to understand what it meant to be touched by him or he wouldn't have made such a big deal about it. In the very next verse it says he placed his hands on them. Perhaps he was telling us that children are capable of understanding much bigger concepts than we give them credit for.

Of course, Wayne and I thought *our children* were always way out there ahead when it came to understanding the big concepts. One of our favorite family stories took place when Dana was eighteen months old. She often visited her grandparents in Wisconsin where every day a siren blew to mark the noon hour. It was loud, and it terrified her and left her screaming. In order to soothe her and help her understand the need for such a loud noise, her preacher grandpa told her it was to let the children know it was time to go home for lunch. He even suggested that Dana say the words, "Go home and get your lunch," each time the whistle blew, which she would do at the top of her little lungs, albeit with the fear of God written all over her face.

One Sunday, our entire family (this included Wayne, his mom, his sister and her family, me, my mother and brother) was packed into the second row of the church, listening to Dad Buchanan deliver his sermon. (He was pretty wound up that day if I remember correctly.) It was a breezy Wisconsin day, and all the church windows were open.

You guessed it! The noon whistle blew, and before we could realize what was happening, Dana stood up in the pew, turned toward the three hundred plus people in the congregation, and shouted, "Go home and get your lunch!"

Do I have to tell you? Church was over at that very moment. No benediction and no seven-fold amen!

Later Dad Buchanan, who had the world's best sense of humor, said, "It wouldn't have been so bad had not half the congregation shouted amen!"

Dear Lord

I pray for all the children in my life. I pray for Matt, Libby, Mary Payton, Lexie, Allie, Andrew, Sarah, Miles, Maggie, and Katie. Don't let them be hindered from your touch. Amen. P.S. Don't let anyone squelch their spontaneity—except maybe in church!

WAYNE! I'M CALLING FROM ROSWELL. WILL YOU ACCEPT THE CHARGES?

All flying insects that walk on all fours are to be detestable to you. There are, however, some winged creatures that walk on all fours that you may eat: those that have jointed legs for hopping on the ground. Of these you may eat any kind of locust, katydid, cricket or grasshopper. But all other winged creatures that have four legs you are to detest.

LEVITICUS 11:20–23

JUST THE MENTION OF locusts makes my skin crawl. About the time you forget there *is* such a thing, they show up again. This was the year! In fact, they just left, at least the ones that didn't die on my front walk.

The Bible says you may eat a locust—ugh! I haven't exactly eaten them, but I've had one jump right in my mouth (talk about spitting!), which is almost as bad as having them jump in your hair. Would you believe I had two in my hair at one time? For a whole day!

All day I kept hearing what sounded like little electric signals, one on each side of my head, almost like two transmitters answering each other. I was sure I'd been abducted by aliens while I was sleeping and they had wired me for their strange purposes. You read about it all the time. You know about Roswell, New Mexico!

That evening when I laid my head back on the chair, the faint noises became a cacophony of sound that sent me straight up and put a spontaneous prayer on my lips: "Oh, dear God, not the space ship. Please not the space ship!"

The verse about bugs in Leviticus shows how minutely concerned God was about the holiness of his people. His servant Moses, through whom he was speaking at the time, wasn't just rattling on about bugs. He was giving God's explicit, detailed instructions as to what the people could eat and what they couldn't. These annoying laws, and a lot more, had to be followed to the letter because sin had to be paid for, worked for! Salvation was at stake!

Thankfully all that work—like figuring out which bug is which—is no longer necessary because of God's gift, his Son, who paid for our sin. Salvation is still at stake, but imagine! It's a gift! The only thing we have to do is accept it.

What in the world was God thinking when he made locusts? And katydids? And salamanders? And elephants? I'm struck that God is not only a God of concern about the holiness of his people but he is a God of detail. And a God of humor. This is another reminder that we can see him and hear his voice in the craziness of everyday life.

Dear Lord

God of all these amazing creatures (including me): How concerned you were about the holiness of your people under the laws of the Old Testament, and yet you are no less concerned about my holiness today under grace. Thank you for concerning yourself with me. Thank you for being a God of detail right down to the buzzer in a locust. For your sweet Son Jesus, I thank you. For salvation! And thank you for being a God of humor in everyday stuff. Amen.

MEN ARE FROM MARS; WOMEN ARE FROM—WHERE IS THAT AGAIN?

God's solid foundation stands firm, sealed with this inscription: The Lord knows who are his.

2 TIMOTHY 2:19

IF YOU SAY THE word "foundation" to a man, he thinks "house"; if you say it to a woman (at least a woman over forty), she thinks "bra."

Wayne can talk forever about how the foundation of our house wasn't done right. He insists the builder forgot to seal it, thus the water problems. I understand that. I use a sealer after I polish my nails, and they last much longer.

For me, the word "foundation" is synonymous with underwear. When I was a preteen my friends and I thought it was a dirty word. When the preacher said, "God was there before the foundation of the earth," we could barely contain ourselves. Our bodies shook convulsively and we rolled our eyes heavenward. In those days, bras were called "foundation garments," and you bought them in a foundations department.

In the olden days, so to speak, bras were not cute frothy lace things hanging from racks on neat little hangers. They were utilitarian! They were in drawers and only "fitters" were trained to measure you and determine which drawer held your size. It was the most mysterious thing you've ever seen. Also the most embarrassing! Your mother would make an appointment and go with you to buy (hesitate and lower voice to a whisper) *foundation garments.*

Much later in history, bras were displayed on tables. Out there for all to see and pointing heavenward, for heaven's sake! By this time, I had children of my own and was no longer embarrassed by them. My daughters were very embarrassed by me, however, and refused to shop with me because of my propensity to walk past a table full of bras and poke them in.

Yes, poke them in! It might be weird, but it's not a sin, you know.

Isn't it funny about our visual images? How two people have such totally opposite frames of reference, see such different pictures in their mind's eye, and yet draw the same conclusions? It must be a "God thing!" Like foundations, for instance. Regardless of your point of view, whether you're talking house or underwear, you're bound to come up with the same adjectives: "Supportive. Sturdy. Sure. Firm!"

We all can understand that "God's solid foundation stands firm." And it's comforting beyond words to know that "the Lord knows who are his," and he won't forget. No siree! I don't think so!

Dear God

Perfect "Builder" of all things: Thank you for a better understanding of you even by means of some very bizarre thought patterns, which are about the only kind I seem to have. Amen.

IT'S A BIRD, IT'S A PLANE, IT'S A FUNERAL HOME!

The wise heart will know the proper time and procedure. For there is a proper time and procedure for every matter.

ECCLESIASTES 8:5–6

SIMPLY PUT, MY TIMING is almost always off! I tend to jump ahead, speak before I think—stick my nose in where it has no business. Open mouth—insert foot! My husband calls it "foot-in-mouth disease."

I certainly didn't get that "disease" from my mother. She was a perfect lady. I can honestly say she was a prime example of knowing the "proper time and procedure for every matter." I only recall once when she stuck her foot in her mouth and was embarrassed by it for the rest of her life.

People had just begun to put double front doors on their houses. It was a new thing, and we knew of only one house that had them. It was the hot topic of conversation—you either liked 'em or you didn't; there was no in between.

Even the newspaper got into the brouhaha. It said that on one hand, it was the latest architectural phenomenon—soon everyone would have them. On the other hand, it said they made many people think of a funeral home. The address of the house with those double front doors was posted in the article, and it was suggested you drive by and make your own judgment. Well, need I tell you, *anybody who was anybody,* got in their cars and high-tailed it over to check it out. Including us!

A few weeks later Mother was introduced to a lady who, in the course of conversation, was trying to tell Mother where she lived. At last, Mother thought she had it. "You must live in the same neighborhood as that house with those horrible double doors. Don't you just think at any moment they'll be coming through with a casket?"

"Actually," the lady said, "I live *in* the house with the horrible double doors."

Mother, if she weren't already dead, would die if she knew I was telling this story. But then again, she had a good sense of humor and by now would be laughing right along with us.

You've said there is a proper time and procedure for every matter. So far today, I've done all right. I haven't gossiped, haven't lost my temper, haven't been greedy, grumpy, nasty, selfish, or over-indulgent. I'm very thankful for that. But, in a few minutes, Lord, I'm going to get out of bed. From then on, I'm probably going to need a lot more help. Amen. P.S. Even though I didn't write this prayer, you know I mean it!

I DON'T CARE FOR YOUR CLOTHES—BUT MY CAT WOULD LOVE THEM!

How good is a timely word!

PROVERBS 15:23

A LOT OF FANCY-SCHMANTZY (and some not so fancy-schmantzy) dress shops have really tried to pick up on that verse lately. Have you noticed that as soon as you walk in the door, regardless of what you look like, you get a compliment? To be sure, it's a sales tactic.

Invariably a sales clerk will tell me my look is "sooo very together," even though I have a gigantic run in my stockings and am wearing only one earring—the other having been left by the phone at the office. Or they'll say my hair is "just fabulous," even when really it's sticking out all over my head and my roots haven't been touched up since Clinton was reelected. These are insincere compliments.

Apparently there is one sales clerk who never got the word that complimenting a customer is good for business. My friend

Joy and I were browsing in a snooty little shop in Miami, when a sales clerk approached us. She looked down her nose (and, frankly, I doubt it was the nose she was born with), sniffed, and said, "Sorry, ladies, we only have small sizes." Well, excuse me! I have a rule never to speak badly about a person unless they have it coming to them; but believe me, this woman had it coming! She may have been a size two, but I promise you she had more than one layer of heavy-duty Lycra on her liposuctioned hips (you could tell by the way she walked and the pained expression on her face), and she was wearing a dress I wouldn't be caught dead in. (Well, the truth is, I'd have to be dead about six months to fit into it!) We were too speechless to answer, much less to think to say that we had daughters who wore small sizes and perhaps we were shopping for them. If I wasn't such a nice person, the perfect answer might have been, "So maybe I like to dress up my cat!"

Then there's the pseudo-compliment, the one that makes me *think* I'm being complimented when I'm not: "My, your sweatshirt is unique." (This is true! It's older than dirt; it says Kelvinator Refrigerators on it.) Or how about, "Your shoes look wonderfully comfortable." (They are! They came over on the ark.)

How about the backhanded compliment? Dana accuses me of delivering those. I say to her, "Your hair really looks good today," and her comeback is, "Didn't it look good yesterday?" Perhaps it's a mother-daughter thing. Now that she's grown up and we're secure with each other (She has and we are, aren't we?) I say, "Your hair looks good; I don't care what anyone says."

Then there's the genuine compliment that comes from a sincere heart. Nobody will turn those down, will they? But wait! We turn them down all the time.

"I love your house!"

"You do? It needs painting—needs new furniture now that the kids are gone."

"This casserole is delicious."

"Heavens, it's nothing. It's nothing more than chicken, cheese, and Campbell's soup."

"Loved your solo at church. It really spoke to my heart."

"You're kidding! I really messed up that last verse."

"I love your dress."

"This thing? Oh, not this dress!"

Years ago I made a beautiful red dress to wear for a Valentine's banquet. I'd worked hard and it fit my young shapely figure quite well, if I do say so myself, although I'd had a little trouble getting it to hang just right. Even so, I felt great in it until the moment I walked into the banquet hall. Then my confidence fell apart.

Suddenly, in this crowd of people I'd never met before, I was sure everyone but me was dressed in a store-bought dress and that my dress didn't measure up. Everyone would not only know my dress was homemade, they would think it *looked* homemade. At the first hint of a compliment I had my comeback ready.

"I made it," I announced. "And look at this, can you believe it? It's crooked. If I stand like this it hangs straight." I exaggerated my shoulders, pushing one high and letting the other drop low.

No one laughed.

"Or maybe it's like this. I forget." I reversed the position of my shoulders.

Still, no one laughed.

"Oh, dear," I babbled. "I can't remember which shoulder should be up and which should be down." By this time I was doing some weird shoulder boogie-woogie—up, down, up, down, up, down—apologizing all over the place for some mythical engineering flaw, and making a fool of myself to boot.

They never laughed. Never even smiled. They nodded and turned away. It's funny now, but it wasn't funny then. And all because I couldn't accept a compliment!

A timely word certainly includes a sincere compliment. It could also be "excuse me" or "thank you" or "I'm sorry." My favorite timely word is "there, there!" Everyone needs a "there, there!" now and then.

Dear Lord

It's about those pseudo-compliments and those backhanded compliments, Lord. Maybe you could work with me on the nasty retorts that are always on the tip of my tongue. Help me stick a sock in it as necessary! I pray that you'll make me more free with my compliments and words of encouragement, pointing out the best in others. Help me say "there, there!" more often. Amen.

YOU'RE NEVER FULLY DRESSED WITHOUT A SMILE ... AND EARRINGS!

Then they (the older women) can train the younger women to love their husbands and children.

TITUS 2:4

SEVERAL TIMES A YEAR my friends and I take off together to work. We are creative women of all ages; some of us write books, some music; others teach and plan school and church productions. These friends not only include Joy, Peggy, and Gloria, but there are other "best friends" too: Lynn, Evelyn, and Marty to name a few.

Several times we've gone to the Cayman Islands. It's hard to concentrate there in such lush surroundings, so we get up at the break of dawn and work for several hours knowing that all day long there will be voices calling. Voices saying, "You shouldn't be working. You should be sailing ... snorkeling ... swimming ... parasailing ... walking the beach ... sunbathing!" You tend to answer those voices: "Yes ... yes ... yes ... I hear you ... I'm coming!"

Other than the time gigantic flying roaches attacked Marty and me and we couldn't run outside because we were in our nighties, and the time the dishwasher overflowed because Peggy put the wrong kind of soap in it and we were up to our knees in suds, our vacations in Cayman have been perfect.

We've not only done Cayman, but we've sailed out of Coconut Grove, Florida, on a beautiful boat called the *Sea Sharpe* that comes complete with captain, and been gone for days at a time. I must say our creativity and productivity is at its peak out there on the ocean in almost total quiet, surrounded by God's handiwork. It's amazing what we've learned from each other as we share our work, our ideas, and our goals. Our voices, singing in harmony, are nothing short of angelic when every night after dinner we sit in our deck chairs, sip our lemonade, and watch a breathtaking sunset.

Our sailing trips have been perfect except for the time the boat caught on fire and we were practically overcome by thick black smoke. We had to go topside and put on life jackets while the captain put the fire out.

As you can imagine, it's not exactly the "all work and no play" we try to make our husbands think it is. Heaven forbid we become dull. When we're on dry land, or in port, we sneak in a shopping trip or two! Or maybe even three!

On one of these occasions we discovered a whole block of street vendors, one of which had *the most* to-die-for, drop-dead gorgeous jewelry we had ever seen. One of my friends—a *much younger girl* who shall remain nameless for obvious reasons—immediately fell in love with a pair of earrings that cost thirty-five *worth-every-cent-of-it* dollars!

"Buy them! Buy them!" we urged, forgetting for the moment that in order to come on this trip, she had to promise her husband (with her hand on her grandmother's Bible) that she wouldn't spend a penny that wasn't absolutely necessary.

"Oh, let me help you. Let me teach you how to deal with these situations," I said. "Buy the earrings, go home, take off all your clothes, put on the earrings and ask your husband if he thinks the expense was *absolutely necessary.*" She bought the earrings, we had a good laugh, and I didn't give it another thought.

The next time I saw her husband, he was grinning from ear to ear. For the life of me I didn't know why. Finally I asked.

"You are a great example of an older woman teaching a younger woman," he said. "My wife can go on a trip with you anytime!"

Girlfriendship can enhance all other relationships. The "getting away" for most women is rarely to an exotic island; it's more likely to be to a church retreat or maybe to the park for a picnic; but this experience—time to compare notes, learn from each other, redefine priorities, and yes, cry on each other's shoulders—invigorates and energizes us to be better wives and mothers.

I often meet women who tell me they would never go off with girlfriends, that they don't do anything apart from their husbands—they are "each other's best friends." But a startling reality, and one that's hard to talk about, is that women are more likely to lose their mate to death than the other way around, and often they have no place to turn and no one to turn to. Many times I meet women in this situation. They've not only lost their *best* friend, but their *only* friend. By then it's too late to have the kind of friends that are developed over a lifetime. Friendship among women provides a "back-up system" that may come in handy when you need it most.

The earring thing is probably not exactly what God had in mind in that exhortation about older women teaching younger women; but on the other hand, maybe it is, at least, a part of it. Sex, and the fun and excitement that goes with it, were, after all, his idea. Perhaps *my approval* will free a younger woman to love her husband with total abandon. And that's a very good lesson!

Dear God

I hate to admit it, but I suppose I qualify as an "older woman." I pray that my younger friends will look up to me and count on me for good advice. Amen.

WHAT'S THAT ABOUT THE POPE'S RING?

*I'm so grateful to Christ Jesus for making
me adequate to do this work. He went out
on a limb, you know, in trusting me with
this ministry. The only credentials I brought
were invective.*

1 TIMOTHY 1:12–13 (THE MESSAGE)

IT'S HARD TO BELIEVE the Lord has trusted me with his ministry.
I haven't looked it up in the dictionary, but I'm sure the meaning of the word "invective" must be "shallow." I'm joking–do I
have to tell you? I know what the word means; I looked it up in
the "bridged" and unabridged both. It means "vehement denun-
ciation; an utterance of violent censure or reproach." There's no
doubt that Christ Jesus really did go out on a limb–I'm talkin'
way out there on a limb–when he allowed me to write books
and be a speaker.

I went through the West Virginia school system when it was
at its worst, and, even then, rarely made grades above a C.
Besides that–and I'm not exactly proud of it–I went to college
for all the wrong reasons. I never let my studies get in the way

of meeting guys and having a good time. Let's just say I was kissed more times than the pope's ring.

Writing for me is strictly "seat of the pants." I barely know a verb from an adverb, and I could as easily draw a map of the back alleys of Bora Bora as I could diagram a sentence. Some might not agree, but I think it's been an advantage to not know these things, because a lot of people are more concerned that their participles might be dangling than about telling a good story. My participles could dangle all day and I'd never know it. Wayne says I also split infinitives. I say, "Only if they need it."

After reading one of the chapters in this book, my daughter Dana called me a "master at non sequiturs." I thanked her for the compliment and began to practice calling myself a "non sequitarian." Then I looked it up. Non sequitur means "a statement or remark that does not follow from the previous conversation." When I confronted her, she said, "But Mother, I love your non sequiturs. They're wonderful; they bounce here, there, and everywhere and turn out just great." Thank you again. *I think?*

As for speaking, it's the scariest thing I've ever done. I almost always get sick beforehand. Each time, I swear I'll never do it again. Added to that, I can't stand the sound of my voice. It's crotchety, exactly like my great aunt Annie's—God rest her soul—and I've never doubted for a minute I'm getting what my mother called my "just deserts." I'm being paid back for making fun of Aunt Annie behind her back!

Then there's the fact that no matter how hard I try, something always goes wrong.

In Chattanooga I was nearly dressed, and it was time to leave my hotel room for my speaking engagement when I discovered I hadn't brought my skirt.

In Pennsylvania I had both top and bottom of my two-piece dress, but, at the very last minute, found the dry cleaners had removed the buttons when they cleaned it and hadn't sewed them back on.

Another time I had what I thought was a pair of black high-heeled pumps, but they weren't a match; one had velvet trim and the other didn't. Then there's the time my slip fell down around my ankles just as I walked in front of the speaker's table.

So talk about going out on a limb! A verse later in that same chapter says, "I'm proof . . . of someone who could never have made it apart from sheer mercy. And now he shows me off . . . evidence of his endless patience . . ." Check out 1 Timothy 1:15–16!

He shows me off! Wow! Pretty amazing under the circumstances!

Dear God

> *If I should ever get too big for my "Victoria's secrets," and start believing my own publicity, help me stop and remember that it says you made me adequate*—not great. *Amen.*

IS IT JUST THE WAY I AM, OR IS IT DUNLAP'S DISEASE?

Just as water mirrors your face, so your face mirrors your heart.

PROVERBS 27:19 (THE MESSAGE)

WHEN I WAS A little girl and my mama would catch me pouting, she would say I'd better be careful or my face would *stick that way*. It wasn't long till I realized there were people in our church—the same ones who griped about the music and the length of the sermon—who might as well have had their unhappy countenances carved into Mount Rushmore; if they had smiled, praised God publicly, or affirmed another person, the roof would have fallen in! I'm afraid their faces mirrored their hearts and stuck that way!

It's funny how you can tell a person's thoughts just by looking at his or her face—or nowadays, by looking at their T-shirts! There seems to be a T-shirt for every personality, every mood, every thought—and yes, every heart! I saw a shirt on a big fat guy that said, "I'm suffering from Dunlap's disease. My stomach dunlaps over my belt." Another said, "Some people are alive simply because it's against the law to kill them." I don't want inside that guy's mind!

There are shirts for the sports minded: "If there's no golf in heaven I'm NOT going." (Gee! We'll miss you!) And for the sportsman's wife: "Give a man a fish and you feed him for a day. Teach a man to fish and you get rid of him for the weekend." (I can actually picture myself in this little number.)

One woman had "male bashing" written on her chest: "*Men*tal breakdown, *men*opause, *men*strual cramps, *men*tal fatigue. Notice how all our problems start with *men*." How about, "Grow your own dope. Plant a man." (I saw it with my own eyes!)

There are shirts that shout "I'm depressed!" without really saying the words. "Due to recent cutbacks, the light at the end of the tunnel has been turned off until further notice."

Some quips make you suck in your breath; they're all too true: "Eat right, live clean, exercise hard, and die anyway!" or "50 is the age of discovery. You discover you are old!"

Then there's the shirt that says, "It's not an attitude. It's the way I am." Sad to say that's true of us all, and there's no doubt about it; it's a heart problem and not just a face problem.

Perhaps there is a remedy that will reverse this "smile stuck in the down position" malady. Maybe watch less TV and read more good books, spend more time with the Lord, read his Word, and meditate on his truths. And buy T-shirts with positive messages, for heaven's sake!

Dear Lord

Maybe today I'll have a shirt made that reads, "Just as water mirrors your face, so your face mirrors your heart." It would be a good reminder. Amen.

MY HUSBAND WOULDN'T BE CAUGHT DEAD WITH A GREEN PEPPER!

Go, eat your food with gladness, and drink
your wine with a joyful heart, for it is now
that God favors what you do.

ECCLESIASTES 9:7

BELIEVE ME, YOU DON'T have to be told to eat your food with gladness around our house! Our friends don't have to be reminded either. As to wine, well that's a touchy subject. A lot of people drink it with a joyful heart but are very secretive about it. I heard someone say (when drink orders were being taken at a restaurant), "We're Baptists; we don't drink in front of one another." It got a good laugh.

Maybe the Bible doesn't really mean wine as we know it today. Maybe in Bible times it was the equivalent of what we call Gatorade. Maybe it was okay back then, but it isn't now. Maybe I should go back to talking about the safe part of that verse—food!

Wayne not only eats with gladness, but he cooks with gladness. It's like I have my very own Chef Boy-ar-dee! In my humble opinion, he takes himself far too seriously in his pursuit, but what do I know? I've only cooked for forty years; *he* started a few years ago.

The process he goes through seems agonizing. First comes a fishing trip with his friend Dan, who is into watching TV cooking shows. The two of them take off on the boat for a couple of days and talk—not women, not football, not even fishing—they talk recipes.

Next there is the rumination period. That's *ruminate*, not *marinade!* Marinade comes later. Sometimes this "thinking about it" takes a week or two, and includes making a list (and perhaps mortgaging the house).

Then comes the shopping experience. "I'll be home late. I'm going grocery shopping." Big deal. I've grocery shopped for forty years and I can't remember having to make an announcement, and they never had to call the police to report me missing. We've come close with Wayne.

"Well, officer, three days ago he went off in search of Cavender's and we haven't seen him since."

"Are you sure there's not another woman?"

"No, officer, I really think it's Cavender's."

Then come the peppers. All of Wayne's recipes begin with peppers: red peppers, yellow peppers, orange peppers, and even purple peppers; never green peppers—too common I suppose. I call him a green pepper snob.

Next is the skinning of the red, yellow, orange, and purple peppers; and, for whatever reason under heaven, *he likes me to watch!*

"C'mere, look at this," he says. "You blanch them in boiling water, and the skin just slides off." Well, duh! Before I could even talk I used to stand on a chair and watch my mother do the same thing.

I must say, when the meal is cooked and the guests arrive, it's worth it. They praise Wayne all the way to heaven and back. They "ooh and aahh" and beg for the recipes.

Last night when the Hodges and Yarboroughs were here for dinner, I not only heard him giving out recipes, but I heard him making a date to show Betsy and Lynn how to remove the skin from peppers.

I have no trouble at all following your suggestion about food— about eating it with gladness and a joyful heart. Thank you for its goodness, its plentiful supply, its variety, and its beauty. Imagine! Peppers in red, yellow, orange, purple, and even (heaven forbid) green! Amen. P.S. Thank you for Wayne's new love of cooking. I have a book deadline!

PARDON MY DRIVING, I'M RELOADING MY GUN. NO, NOT RELOADING MY GUN—PRAYING! THAT'S IT, I'M PRAYING!

Be joyful always; pray continually.

1 Thessalonians 5:16–17

THE LORD MUST HAVE had busy women in mind when he said to pray continually. We have to pray continually just to get through the day! It's a good thing God didn't say we had to stop five times (or seven, or even once), run to the bedroom, and get down on our knees by the bed, or our prayers wouldn't count. If he had, most of us wouldn't do it. Another thing! He must have taken into consideration the fact that while we were off praying, our kids would be off killing each other!

I think I'm a pretty good example of someone who prays continually. When I'm cooking, I like to pray for those who will be eating the food, and please don't take that the wrong way. I'm a very good cook. (I do *not* use the smoke alarm as a timer!) It's just that what better time to pray for your dinner guests than while you're preparing their food?

Another place I pray is in the car. "Dear Lord: Please bless my—*hey you, get in your own lane*—family. Please give me an understanding of your Word, and a sweet—*Yo man, slow down!*—spirit."

When I watch TV, I sometimes pray for the people on the shows. "Dear God: Help—*oooh, he's so cute*—Stone Phillips!"

I especially pray for the people on those shows where they yell, scream, confront, and beat each other up. No, wait! You're taking it the wrong way. *I only watch so I can pray more intelligently!*

Unless I'm misinterpreting the verse, and heaven knows it wouldn't be the first time I've misinterpreted a verse, I think it's implying that praying continually will make us joyful. It occurs to me that if I'm *really* praying continually, then maybe this attitude of joy will spill over into my activities and behaviors, and maybe even back into my prayers!

Let's talk. Continually! You are there with me wherever I am, so why not? And please, fill my life with joy! Amen.

WHO SAID RATTLESNAKES DON'T HAVE DISCERNMENT?

*Come, let us sing for joy to the LORD; let us
shout aloud to the Rock of our salvation. Let
us come before him with thanksgiving and
extol him with music and song.*

PSALM 95:1–2

DOES IT SEEM THERE are a disproportionate number of verses in
the Bible about singing? Am I the only one who feels picked on?
I have a terrible voice.

When I was a teenager I could sing. I sang in a trio that
traveled all over West Virginia and beyond. The trio members,
Janet, Carlene, and I, along with Susie, who took my place when
I went off to college, are still the greatest of friends to this day.
One of the highlights of each year is when the four of us get
together for a reunion. We laugh! We cry! Sometimes we sing
right straight through the hymn book without stopping! Always
we reminisce about the episodes of our youth, our favorite being
that of the *great greasy goose*.

We had driven for miles to sing at a youth banquet in a
dank, drab, crepe-paper-draped church basement. It should have

been a clue that something was amiss when, immediately upon our arrival, we were pulled aside and told to "act naturally no matter what happens, and don't ask questions."

While we were rehearsing, trying to get used to the ancient, out-of-tune, beat-up old piano, we couldn't help noticing a teenage boy sobbing like his heart was broken. Those around him were making an effort, but no one seemed to be able to console him.

There was an air of anticipation as the banquet began. Not necessarily a *positive* air of anticipation, but nevertheless anticipation! We were seated, the blessing was said, and there was a pall-like silence—like in a funeral home when a favorite uncle has died. No one moved a muscle. At last the kitchen door gave a great "whoosh," and through it came a very determined-looking woman balancing—on one hand held high in the air as though she was the head chef at the Waldorf Astoria—the biggest platter you've ever seen.

On it was ... the biggest ... the biggest ... what? Turkey? No! Too big for a turkey! Let's just say it was the biggest *bird of unknown origin* we'd ever seen. It was practically meatless; its ribs stood like a snow fence on a winter's day, and the puddle it reclined in contained more grease than Elvis Presley's pompadour. With great ceremony, the platter was placed on the head table in front of us, and carved right under our noses, for heaven's sake!

The crying got louder—now everybody in the room was crying—but somehow dinner and the program continued as though everyone was in their right mind, which they weren't, of course. Only moments before our trio was introduced someone came forward and gave a lovely speech, thanking the selfless young man, who was now smiling through his tears, for contributing his pet 4-H blue-ribbon goose to the youth dinner! There was a round of applause, a standing ovation, and it was time for us to sing.

"Some glad morning when this life is o'er ... !" The words were barely out of our mouths when we began to pinch each other—we always stood with our arms around each other and pinched if there was a problem. There was—due to the very inappropriate next line of the song—and we were pinching each other senseless! What could we do? It was too late to go back!

"I'll fly away," we sang to a fresh round of tears.

Fortunately, sometimes you can't tell the difference between laughing and crying. Our bodies were shaking convulsively all the way through our first stand and tears were running down our faces like rivers. Just about the time we'd begin to recover, we would glance down at that greasy carcass—which, by the way, stayed on the table till long after the benediction was pronounced—and we would "lose it" again. Afterward everyone thanked us for being so sensitive and caring. Perhaps they thought of our ill-chosen song as a tribute!

We performed at many an all-day-dinner-on-the-grounds, dozens of family reunions, and more church services than we could count, of every persuasion imaginable, including one that handled snakes. Fortunately, the snakes didn't come out the day we sang. I doubt it was anything personal, but then again, maybe it was.

I'm thankful for the experience of singing in that trio, but I must tell you, my singing days are over. I can whistle beautifully—in tune and on pitch—and I don't like to brag, but I can do a rendition of "Trumpet Voluntary" (better known as Princess Diana's wedding song) like nothing you've ever heard, but there just doesn't seem to be much of a demand for whistlers.

"Hey, Sue, how about joining the church whistlers? We could use someone with your talent." Or, "Would you check July of 2004 and see if you could possibly whistle for our convention?" *I don't think so!*

Psalm 33:1 says, "Sing joyfully to the Lord," and I'm wondering, if not joyfully, maybe *enthusiastically?* Even though I can't carry a tune in a large bucket with a lid on it, I've learned that if I stand in the middle of a group of real honest-to-goodness singers, look enthusiastic, and mouth the words (and move like Tina Turner), people think I can sing.

Last Christmas a group of these real honest-to-goodness musicians went Christmas caroling and I was invited to go along. We had just made our rounds at a local hospital when the TV cameras showed up. Later on the ten o'clock news, there I was smack-dab front and center, mouthing the words to the Christmas songs for dear life as the newswoman proclaimed, "Tonight, Nashville's very finest singers took time out of their busy schedules ... blah, blah, blah, etc., etc., etc."

Another time we had a birthday party for a friend, a Nashville music executive, and I was asked to help write a song (I *can* do that) for the occasion. Later at the party, we sang it accompanied by a live band. Again I found myself surrounded by some of "Nashville's finest." Again I enthusiastically mouthed the words and performed like there was no tomorrow. Afterward, those who didn't know the truth showered me with praise, saying they had no idea I was such a great singer.

Thank you very much. Autographs anyone?

When they were little, Dana and Mindy were in a group called "The Sunday School Picnic." They sang on almost every children's record that was produced in Nashville at that time, from Gaither projects (Do you remember the song, "I Am a Promise; I Am a Possibility"?) to those of Word, Benson, Broadman, and United Methodist Publishing House. The group was even featured on "The Jimmy Dean Show" and the stage of the Grand Old Opry. Mindy went on to become a top child talent, singing and sometimes performing on jingles and commercials that were aired nationwide. I was a proud mama and Wayne was a proud daddy. We loved to hear our children sing! We loved the sound of their voices!

And just think! God loves to hear his children sing. He loves the sound of my voice. Even though I can't carry a tune, God hears my raspy, out-of-tune voice. It's music to his ears, and it brings him glory. He loves the sound of your voice in praise, too. How long has it been since he has heard it?

Dear Lord

God in heaven: This singing thing seems to be a really big issue with you. I'll do my best! If not with my voice, oh God, then with my heart. Let my heart *sing out even in the quiet of the night, knowing you hear my song. Or maybe I'll just* mouth *the words—a silent "shout" to the Rock of my salvation. Occasionally, I suppose, I could go ahead and just belt it out—let loose! It's not a pretty sound, but maybe I can do it in the shower, or alone in the car, or out in the forest. I'll do it because you said, "Sing!" And I am your child, and you love the sound of my voice! Amen.*

YOU CAN'T PUT M&MS IN ALPHABETICAL ORDER, CAN YOU?

Test me, O LORD, and try me, examine my heart and my mind; for your love is ever before me, and I walk continually in your truth.

PSALM 26:2–3

I'VE BEEN TOLD STRAIGHT out that I should have my head examined, but until I read Psalm 26 I never thought about asking God to examine it. From the theme of this book you already know that I'm teased about being ditzy. And shallow. And blonde! There isn't a week goes by that someone doesn't send me a list of blonde jokes.

Sue is so blonde . . .

- . . . she tried to put M&Ms in alphabetical order.
- . . . she tripped over a cordless phone.
- . . . she spent thirty minutes looking at the orange juice can because it said "concentrate."
- . . . she studied for her blood test and failed.
- . . . she sold her car for gas money.

... when she heard that 95 percent of all crimes occur near your home, she moved.

By the way, do you know why blonde jokes are short? Well, duh! It's so men can understand them!

I'm not very politically correct; I don't mind being *teased* about being a dumb blonde. It's being *treated* like a dumb blonde I don't like! We once had a client whose business I'd worked hard to get. We'd met several times at his office, and I'd offered workable solutions for his company's needs. We'd agreed on a plan of action, and I'd even developed a detailed budget and plan for implementation.

"Hey, I'll come to your office next time," he said as we shook hands. The very next day he did just that; he walked in, stopped at my office door, greeted me effusively, then ushered himself into my husband's office and announced, "Sue's been a big help. Now we're ready to go. Let's get started."

My husband was flabbergasted. He knew very little about the project. We had an unspoken agreement that it was in the best interest of our business that we not try to share accounts; we would each tend to our own. We also understood that there were those who preferred to work with him, and those who preferred to work with me, and we tried to honor that and not get in each other's way. That particular time I was pretty steamed, but Wayne went ahead with the account. Today we might handle it differently—I'm a little more confrontational! I can play the dumb blonde to the hilt when I'm in the mood, but I don't much like it pushed down my throat.

When God implies that we need to have our heads examined, he isn't talking about checking for blonde hair or brilliance (thank heavens); he's looking for a person whose commitment is to "walk continually in [God's] truth."

Continually! Not occasionally, not most of the time. It's a full-time thing!

Dear Lord

Help me walk in your truth and in your love. Continually! *Examine my heart. Examine my head. Continually. Amen.*

THIS HAPPENED LONG BEFORE BATH AND BODY SHOPS

> *When they enter the gates of the inner court,*
> *they are to wear linen clothes; they must not*
> *wear any woolen garment while ministering*
> *at the gates of the inner court or inside the*
> *temple.*
>
> EZEKIEL 44:17

I KNOW THAT EZEKIEL 44:17 is talking about priests and how they should dress inside the temple, and I know there was a reason they shouldn't wear wool. But for the life of me, I can't remember what it was.

But I can tell you wool itches! And I can tell you that having a bunch of scratching, itching priests leading worship could be pretty doggone distracting. Picture it if you will, keeping in mind that the severity of the itch is proportional to the difficulty of the reach!

Due to the primitive bathing conditions they had in those days, there must have been a lot of itching and scratching going on anyway. And think of the odors! Not just body odors, but there were animals everywhere. You've seen the pictures in Bible story books. Some were being sacrificed, for heaven's sake! Burnt offerings? Phew! I hate the smell of *burnt toast.*

Add to that the food smells. People seemed to just squat right there in the courtyard, build a fire, and cook! (I'm only going by the pictures, mind you.) And remember, there was no refrigeration.

Mix all of the above with that strange, sickening odor from the incense pots, and the stench from the other kind of squatting, if you know what I mean. The sum total of it had to be nause-ating! Remember, not only did all this take place before those lit-tle country garden plug-ins, it was before electricity!

It was also long before Jesus Christ came to earth to bring us grace. Grace that would free us and do away with the con-fining laws. Who God *is* hasn't changed a smidgen. He is the same yesterday, today, and forever, and his holiness requires— even demands!—the same awe and reverence that was expected in the Old Testament. The laws that were laid down to the priests of old were just a small piece of a much bigger picture.

Dear Lord

Sometimes we behave in your presence in a more flippant way than we would in the presence of some earthly dignitary. Make us aware of your holiness. It seems we ask and ask and ask, and then we demand *that our wants and our pleasures be ful-filled. We say, "I'll do this, if you'll do that." Instead, let our prayers be formed on our faces against a backdrop of your majesty, praying, "Not my will but yours." Amen.*

REPLACEMENT PARTS AND OTHER TECHNO-WONDERS OF THE MODERN AGE

I praise you because I am fearfully and wonderfully made; your works are wonderful, I know that full well.

PSALM 139:14

ARE WE REALLY "FEARFULLY made?" Yep, and if I doubt it, all I have to do is look in the mirror first thing in the morning. A scary sight! There's a line in a hymn that says, "Look ye saints, the sight is glorious." Hmmmm, not in my mirror! At least not before Maybelline!

Not too many of us sit around and think about the fact that we are wonderfully made. In fact, quite the opposite is true. We complain about our bodies continually—that we're too fat, or our hips are too big, or our breasts are too small or they sag.

Mine will never sag! After breast cancer I had reconstructive surgery, so even after everything else goes to pot, my techno-breasts will remain perfect. Someday they'll dig up my body—decayed beyond recognition—and there they'll be, still pointing heavenward! In my case, the verse could read " . . . fearfully and *artificially* made"!

Not long after I had my overhaul (so to speak) and was still feeling very body-conscious, I had an important client meeting. It not only included several representatives from the company I was producing for, but several equipment suppliers as well. I wasn't just on the spot to come up with workable ideas, but I was in charge of leading the meeting and responsible to negotiate a win-win situation for everyone.

That morning I dressed carefully. I put on my new electric-blue pantsuit Wayne had bought me in Chicago—*my very fashionable, and in my opinion, quite stunning electric-blue pantsuit*—the drama of which was in the draping effect of the neckline. It could be worn two ways depending on the mood. You could wear it with a blouse or camisole and leave the neckline open; or you could wear it (I thought) without a blouse and pull the draping to one shoulder and attach it to a large, asymmetrical button. This particular morning I made the without-the-blouse choice.

The meeting went well at first, but somewhere along the way the negotiations with one of the vendors broke down. We simply couldn't come to an agreement. At last, in frustration (and for effect), I stood to my feet, smacked the table with my palm, put my hands on my hips, and said, "I'm sorry. This just isn't working for me."

Wow! My theatrics seemed to be working better than I'd hoped! Everyone came to attention like a precision drill team; shoulders straightened, chins dropped, and mouths flew open. Then, just as I was mentally patting myself on the back for being so savvy in my leadership skills, all eyes (eyes that seemed to be popping out of their sockets, I might add) shifted from my face to my chest. My eyes followed their gaze. When I saw what they saw, I thought I would die right then and there. One whole side of me—albeit covered in a black lace bra and draped in electric blue—had popped out for the world to see!

The room got so quiet you could have heard an ant breathing. Finally, one of the men broke the silence. He turned to the others, put on the silly face he knew would get the laugh he was after, and said, "Well, it sure is working for me."

In Ephesians 2:10 it says that "we are God's workmanship." Another translation uses the word "masterpiece." I certainly wasn't thinking about being God's masterpiece that memorable day. I laughed with the others, but I must say I was more than slightly embarrassed.

But think about it! I'm a masterpiece! You're a masterpiece! Isn't that another reason for us to compliment each other—even be lavish with our praise? After all, we are praising God when we do that. And if others say good things about us and we twist and squirm, uneasy with being complimented, well duh! We are denying our Father his just worship.

"You are God's child; you are beautiful; you are talented; you are a true gift to my life!"

Oh, thank you! Thank you very much! And likewise!

Dear God

Even with replacement parts and extra pounds around the middle, I'm still quite remarkable because you made me. Help me spend more time praising you for your handiwork and less time complaining. And may I learn to accept compliments as gifts, as treasures, knowing that my attributes and talents come from you. Amen.

MY COMPUTER HAS MEMORY, AND SOMETIMES I THINK IT'S HOLDING A GRUDGE

You were taught, with regard to your former way of life, to put off your old self, which is being corrupted by its deceitful desires; to be made new in the attitude of your minds.

EPHESIANS 4:22–23

WHEN I THINK OF "old versus new," I think of a computer. It's like we lived in the dark ages before computers. In the last few years we've had to throw out practically everything we knew about anything, and start all over using this new technology. It's been like going from the horse to the Model T. From walking down a path in the dirt to jumping on a super highway—the information highway! Everyone from grandmothers who want to send e-mail to their grandchildren, to those responsible for medical diagnostics and missile defense, has had to learn to "put off the old and be made new" when it comes to gathering and communicating information.

Everything uses computer chips: from household appliances like coffee pots, to cameras, to cell phones, to beepers. My husband loves his beeper. It has several settings: three different audible sounds, a vibrating signal, or no signal where you just keep checking to see if you have a message. Wayne prefers the vibrating signal. It causes him to jump like he's being electrocuted; apparently it feels good. I can sit down at my computer, type a message to him through Skytel and before you can blink an eye, he jumps out of his skin, checks his beeper, and knows whether to bring home toilet paper or Chinese food (no, there's no connection!).

Even automobiles are run by computers. My friend Judy has the smartest car I've ever met. Not only does it have all the fancy-schmantzy accoutrements of a loaded Cadillac Eldorado, but it has a few other computerized features as well. One night last winter after a Christmas party, we found ourselves lost just outside of Nashville.

"Don't worry," she said; "my car knows exactly where we are."

"Your car knows where you are?" I asked.

"Yes," she answered, "something to do with the computer."

"Well, I understand computer memory," I said, "but the car has never been here before."

Before you could say super-cyber-space six times—and while still driving sixty miles an hour through a residential neighborhood, I might add—Judy had punched a few buttons and had the answer.

"Hey, we could've ridden with Mark and sent your car home on its own," I muttered.

Not only did her car tell us we were in Madison, Tennessee, but that we were pointed north. It told us the name of the street we were on and the intersection we were near. It gave us directions to the interstate, and even knew our latitude and longitude. In our case that wasn't important, but just think! If we were missionaries in the middle of a jungle, say in Brazil, it would be a different story. But then again, missionaries usually don't drive Cadillac Eldorados.

Judy went on to say "If I park my car at the airport and forget to lock it, I can call a number and it will lock it for me—or unlock it. Or even find it if I lose it."

Judy's car is so smart she doesn't need a husband, and if she had a husband, most of the features wouldn't be needed. Would a husband ask *a car* for directions? I don't think so!

God wants us to put off our old selves and start anew. He wants us to be made new in the attitude of our minds. Perhaps we're like Judy's car in that there is upkeep involved. For the upkeep on her car there are oil changes and lube jobs, it needs to be washed and swept out, and it needs to have gas in it. It can't run on Kool-Aid, for heaven's sake! Our upkeep includes reading God's Word, praying, being with other believers, going to church, and singing his praises.

Dear Lord

Help me put off my old self to be made new in the attitude of my mind. In other words, delete my corrupted program and wipe the screen of my mind clean to begin anew. Amen.

THANKS FOR CALLING, BUT I'M NO LONGER DOING MOTHER-DAUGHTER BANQUETS

Listen, my son, to your father's instruction
and do not forsake your mother's teaching.
They will be a garland to grace your head
and a chain to adorn your neck.

PROVERBS 1:8

WE ALL KNOW THAT in the Bible the word *son* also means *daughter;* the word is interchangeable. It's just that the writers of the Bible weren't as politically correct as we are now.

Once when I was preparing to speak for a mother-daughter banquet I asked my daughters what tidbits of wisdom I'd taught them that I could pass on to others. Big mistake!

"Tell them to snap out of it," Dana said in the shrill tone of voice she saves for me and me alone. "That's what you told me all my life. I'm in a permanent state of snap-out-of-it-ness. It's imbedded in my brain. I can see it now on my tombstone; 'Here lies the body of Dana; she died trying to *snap out of it.*' Mother, puh-leeze! Get a life! I'm not made of foam rubber!"

Sorry I asked!

"Tell them to say the 'magic word,' and to mind their Ps and Qs," was Mindy's answer. "And tell them if they don't, you'll knock their teeth down their throats. That's what you told me."

Sorry again! But it's true.

I had invited a rather proper older friend to go to lunch at a fancy little tea room and thought it would be okay to take three-year-old Mindy along—she always behaved impeccably. At least in the past she had always behaved impeccably. For some reason that day, though, she was acting terrible and was driving me crazy. All the way there, she hung over the seat whining and fussing; and all the way there, I was feeling the disapproving glances of my guest.

I could see I needed to take some sort of action fast or lunch would be a disaster. When we got out of the car (we were fortunate to find a place to park right in front), I grabbed Mindy by the arm, pulled her close (well okay, *jerked* her close), and said—in her ear, and through tightened lips—"If you don't straighten up, I'm going to knock your teeth down your throat." (You must believe me! This is absolutely the only time in my life I ever said such a thing to either one of my daughters.)

Mindy looked up at me with horror written all over her innocent little face, but with all the drama of a Hollywood actress, and loudly emoted: "You're (sob) going to knock my (sob) teeth down my throat? Oh, Mama (sob) please ... puh-leeze don't knock my teeth down my throat. (sob) I'll be good. I promise, I'll   be good."

About then I turned, not only to see the look of horror on my guest's face, but to meet the stares of twenty or so elegantly dressed ladies as well—mouths open, forks suspended in mid-air—who were lunching in the outdoor courtyard of the restaurant. Is there a travel agent for guilt trips?

A mother can't win. I once visited Dana's high school wearing a suede suit; her friends (the boys) said, "Who's the foxy chick?" Dana was embarrassed out of her mind: "Why can't you dress like the other mothers?" When I wore jeans and an old T-shirt, she said, "Moth-ER. Why are you dressed like that?" If

I drove the big car, she said, "Don't drive that; they'll think we're rich." If I drove the small car, she said, "Do you want them to think we're poor?" You really can't win!

If you only knew how hard I tried with those girls! I washed, I ironed, and I cleaned till my fingers were bloody. I picked up underwear from the floor, I made cookies (I washed my hands in between), sewed clothes, drove hook-ups, went on field trips, and did without so they could have nice things. Life just isn't fair! At least for mothers.

Dear Lord

Please let my daughters remember the good things I taught them (and I know they do). Things about you! Let them remember, and thoroughly enjoy, the crazy things as well, and smile for years to come in the remembering. Amen.

IT'S A NEW SPECIES: PART MAN, PART BARCOLOUNGER!

He who finds a wife finds what is good and receives favor from the Lord.

PROVERBS 18:22

NO OFFENSE, LORD, BUT Proverbs 18:22 may not always be true. I've known several cases where a man found a wife and it was a bad thing—a very bad thing! There have been stories in the news about wives doing dreadful things to their husbands.

Even in our own case (though I've never been known to do bodily harm, unlike some of those women in the news articles), there have been times Wayne has questioned whether finding a wife was such a good thing. One of those times might be when he wants to watch a ballgame on TV *for the millionth time* and I don't want him to.

From a wife's perspective, "watching a game" is synonymous with "sleeping through a game," and sleeping includes snoring, groaning, drooling, and twitching. Wives understand that even though the viewer is asleep, the television must be turned up to the highest possible decibel level. And we know, having learned our lesson the hard way, that if you turn the TV down or off during said game, the viewer wakes up and acts as though the Lord has returned and he's missed it—and it's *your* fault!

I'll admit I'm high maintenance and need a lot of attention, and I know it can't be fun and games all the time—even playing Twister in your underwear can get old if you do it every night! But another ballgame? Puh-leeze! I've heard that Elvis Presley was known to pull out a gun and riddle the TV screen with bullets. Let me put it this way: It's a good thing I don't carry a gun!

I do have my secret ways, however, to punish Wayne— whoops, make that *tease* Wayne—and entertain myself on game nights, which with cable seems to be every night of the week.

Dizzy, our yellow cat, loves to stretch out on Wayne's leg and wrap her little paws around his thigh as he watches TV. After both are asleep, I've discovered that if I talk to Dizzy in a certain tone of voice, it will make her so happy she'll "make bread" with her paws and dig into Wayne's leg with her claws.

"Dizzy, you're a pretty little cat," I say, and her paws start moving. Wayne winces! I wait a little while and begin again. "Dizzy, Dizzy, look at you, such a sweet kitty." She digs! Wayne winces and jerks! "Dizzy, you're such a happy kitty. Such happy little paws." Wayne is practically in spasms, but he doesn't wake up. Sometimes this goes on for a very long time. Sometimes it's my entertainment for the entire evening. Sometimes Wayne wakes up and makes popcorn.

Sometimes I'm as mean as a snake! Help me! Amen.

WHERE I COME FROM, A LITTLE DEBBIE SNACK CAKE IS A VEGETABLE

> *One man's faith allows him to eat every-*
> *thing, but another man, whose faith is*
> *weak, eats only vegetables. The man who*
> *eats everything must not look down on him*
> *who does not, and the man who does not eat*
> *everything must not condemn the man who*
> *does, for God has accepted him.*
>
> ROMANS 14:2–3

I LOVE IT WHEN God and I see eye to eye. I'm glad it's not *my* faith that's weak. My faith allows me to eat everything and any-thing. I do know some vegetarians, though. In fact, I know one vegetarian who is very self-righteous about her diet. (This isn't gossip, I'm simply reporting.) By her own admission she's *theeee* most wonderful Christian in town; she can quote the Bible backward and forward and back again. In fact, to hear her tell it, you'd think she was *born* with a Bible in her hand, which must have been painful for her mother.

Not only is she the epitome of "church lady," but she has this Barbie-esque figure—people who are vegetarians are always skin-nier than others—and contrary to what you've been told, skinny women die at a younger age than fat women. (It's because fat women kill them!)

To me, vegetarians sometimes look anorexic—and their skin is sallow. And while I never thought of it until you pointed it out, Lord, it's obvious their faith is shallow, or they'd trust you to take care of them when they eat all that highly processed red meat. I would never look down on these people, but really! Can you imagine choosing arugula and radicchio over biscuits with sausage and gravy?

Dear Lord

Thank you that I'm not like other people. Wait! Where have I heard that before? Me, self-righteous? Help! Amen.

YOU HAVE THE RIGHT TO REMAIN SILENT; ANYTHING YOU SAY WILL BE MISQUOTED AND HELD AGAINST YOU

Words satisfy the mind as much as fruit does the stomach; good talk is as gratifying as a good harvest.

PROVERBS 18:20 (THE MESSAGE)

IF I COULD GO back to school and start again, I would study the origin of words and phrases. It's only been in the last five or six years that I've learned to love words and understand that they can truly satisfy your mind, even if it's just in the fun and games of it.

I love mind-bogglers like this one: If lawyers are *disbarred* and clergymen *defrocked,* doesn't it follow that electricians could be *delighted,* musicians *denoted,* cowboys *deranged,* models *deposed,* and dry cleaners *depressed?* Wouldn't you expect laundry workers to *decrease,* eventually becoming *depressed* and *depleted?* Won't all composers one day *decompose* and all politicians be *devoted?*

As for where phrases come from, I loved finding out that Hershey's Kisses are called that because the machine that makes them looks like it's kissing the conveyor belt.

I wasn't quite as excited to find out that the nursery rhyme "Ring Around the Rosy" was *not* the sweet platitude I thought it was. I pictured chubby-cheeked children dancing around a rose bush till they got dizzy and fell into a heap of tickles and giggles. Instead, I found that it was written during the outbreak of bubonic plague and was speaking about the red infectious, circular sores ("ring around the rosy") that came with the illness. These sores would smell bad, so people would put flowers somewhere on their bodies (often in their pockets) to cover the smell of the sores ("pocket full of posies").

Well, yuck! I could have gone the rest of my life not knowing that! But since we've gone this far, I'm sure you're wondering about "Ashes, ashes. All fall down." Those who died were burned to ashes to reduce the spread of the disease! Sorry! You asked! No more "Ring Around the Rosy" at my parties. It's back to Twister!

Dear Lord

Thank you, heavenly Father, for words—satisfying words! (Help us turn off the TV and read, for heaven's sake!) For books: nursery rhymes, biographies, poetry, librettos, who-done-its, and your very own message to us all, the Bible! Thank you for conversation—good talk—around the table, on the phone, in the car, in restaurants, in the park, wherever. Amen. P.S. Thank you for silly stuff. That's pretty satisfying for some of us! Probably not for everybody!

YOU PAID FOR YOUR PLANE TICKET; MAKE SURE YOU GET YOUR MONEY'S WORTH!

My command is this: Love each other as I have loved you. Greater love has no one than this, that he lay down his life for his friends.

JOHN 15:12–13

LAYING DOWN MY LIFE for a friend isn't something I'd be eager to do, and although I have wonderful, loyal friends, I doubt they are sitting around waiting to lay down their lives for me. I do, however, have friends who make me fall down laughing, if that counts.

Everything my "just out of college" friend Phillip sends me is funny. His sole purpose in life seems to be to keep me laughing. He's always sending me things in the mail (he's been known to address the envelope to The Reverend Sue Buchanan or The Reverend Mother Sue Buchanan). My favorite Phillip composition came when I first began to take speaking engagements. It was called, "Airport Rules for Divas."

- The rules about carry-on luggage don't apply to you. If there is an emergency landing in the desert, you must have access to a sleeveless shorts outfit with high-heeled sandals. A wide-brimmed hat would be nice in case you're interviewed on TV. For a mountain crash landing you'll need a fur-lined parka with hat and fur-lined boots to match. In the case of a water landing, a one-piece swimsuit with a matching cover-up thrown over your arm is a must, along with a large economy-size tube of shark repellent. You can't possibly fit all this into one small carry-on.

- When the captain makes the announcement about descending, don't let him rush you. If you aren't finished with your makeup, hit the call button and have him circle till you're finished.
- When they make the announcement about seat-backs and tray tables, it doesn't mean you. If your makeup is spread out, take all the time you need, honey. When they say to turn off all portable electronics, it doesn't apply to your lighted vanity mirror, curling iron, or blow-dryer.
- When the arrival gate has been determined, have the captain call ahead for soft lighting. You don't want to look like a deer caught in the headlights when you make your entrance.
- Remember, the concourse at the airport is a natural runway. Wear sunglasses and a scarf and *work it, girl!* Two, three, four, and turn!

Dear Lord

Thank you again and again for friends like Phillip who will go out on a limb—do something totally off the wall—to make me laugh. At the moment, I really don't need someone to lay down his life, but I sure do need to laugh. Amen.

IS THERE A GREETING CARD FOR A BAD HAIR DAY?

Peace be with you!

JOHN 20:21

IN BIBLE TIMES, PEOPLE didn't send cards, but they certainly were into greetings! Greetings like "The Lord be with you! The Lord bless you!" (Ruth 2:4); "Long life to you! Good health to you and your household" (1 Samuel 25:6); and "Peace to this house" (Luke 10:5), to name a few.

Nowadays, there's a greeting card for everything, and the name of the game is specificity. The card doesn't just say "Happy Birthday." It has to say exactly *which* birthday. It's okay when you're ten, and it's even funny when you're over-the-hill forty. But puh-leeze! Enough is enough!

There are bar mitzvah cards, first communion cards, and even "sorry about your divorce" cards. The other day I saw a new category. It said: "Where do I stand with you?" and was for someone who had apparently had a date or two and was anxious to see if the other person wanted to get serious. I'd call that "pushing the envelope."

Speaking of being specific, how about the following:

You're always complaining, you continually cry.
We're sick of listening, so get over it *or die!*

Yes, the haircut is bad. You have my deep sorrow.
But if it is a help, I've a wig you can borrow.

My tire was thumping, I thought it was flat;
When I looked at the tire, I noticed your cat.
So sorry!

You've had your bladder removed, you're now on the
    mends;
Here's a bouquet of flowers and a box of Depends.
Get well soon!

(The last two are not original; they came from one of my crazy e-mail friends.)

Cards—even the ones you make at home—are not only a great way to keep in touch with those you love, but they're a sure way to "grow" new friendships. A good way to say, "Peace be with you!" The funny cards can't be beat, but with all my heart I look forward to the thoughtful ones—those that come with a blessing.

Did you ever notice how often a person comes into your thoughts for seemingly no reason at all? I've begun to realize there's a good chance it's not some crazy fluke, but instead it's one of God's "nudges." He's saying that the person you are thinking of needs a word of encouragement, a visit, a phone call, a note. Maybe a silly handmade greeting card! God isn't hitting us over the head with a two-by-four, he's just nudging us.

Just recently I received a card from a lady I've never met. Inside was a letter thanking me for blessing her life through my writing. She said it made her feel like I was her close friend, shar-ing fears, pain, joy, and a sense of humor. "God just wants to use ordinary people to touch the world for him, doesn't he?" she remarked. She is so right! She ended by adding, "You have touched my life, Sue Buchanan, and I want you to know that I love and appreciate you. God bless, and bless, and bless you!"

Dear Lord

How in the world did Alice from Hubbard, Ohio, know how much I needed her blessing—your blessing, Lord—and how did it happen to come on the exact *day I needed it? Was it what I think it was? Oh Lord, I want to be responsive to your nudges—those times when you put your elbow in my ribs and say,* "Do *something, girl! I don't care what you do. Just do* something!" *Amen.*

THAT TWO-PIECE RED OUTFIT YOU'RE WEARING IS LOVELY, BUT IT NEEDS A GOOD IRONING

You are familiar with all my ways. Before a word is on my tongue you know it completely, O LORD.

PSALM 139:4 (THE MESSAGE)

DO I UNDERSTAND PSALM 139:3–4 correctly? I don't have a clue as to what I might say next, but before a word is on my tongue, *he knows it?* Talk about scary! And still, knowing what he knows, he sends me out there as a speaker—as his representative?

I'd quit speaking publicly tomorrow if it weren't for the fact I love the opportunity it provides to travel around the country and collect new "old friends." If the truth be known, I can't wait to finish speaking so I can talk one-on-one; it never ceases to amaze me how strongly you can bond with a person even though you have only a few minutes together. Whether it's a word of affirmation, a joke, a prayer request, or a life story in a nutshell, I feel privileged to share a few private moments with these friends.

The theme of my message (and I use the term loosely) is that I spent a lot of years thinking I had to change my whole persona in order to make God happy with me. I thought he couldn't possibly want a wacky, offbeat—even shallow—person like me representing his interests. But, surprise, surprise! He does! And surprise, surprise again! Half the people I meet are every bit as wacky and offbeat and shallow as I am. "After hearing you speak ..." they say, followed by a huge pause that hangs in the air like cigar smoke at a poker game. (Now there's a perfect example of not knowing what I might say next. I've never in my life played poker—at least not while smoking a cigar.) "After hearing you speak ..." they say. *Eeeeeeek!* I'm thinking, *Here it comes!* I'm bracing myself! "I've decided, I'm just like you. I'm crazy!" *Oh, you poor soul!* But here's the clincher; here's what makes it all worthwhile: "It never dawned on me before that it's okay to be crazy—okay for me to be *me*—that I can be crazy and still be God's person." *Wow! It took me years to learn that.*

Sadly, many women (and men too) I meet are managing to mask their very spirit so they'll feel accepted by their church friends. After speaking in California recently I received a letter from one of my new "old friends," June.

"I've read your book *I'm Alive and the Doctor's Dead*, and I'm delighted with your sense of humor," she wrote. "I have one too but I have to watch where I use it. Today in our Bible study the question was asked, 'What does it mean to stand fast?' I said, 'It means to stand up in a hurry.' No one laughed or even thought it was funny. See, sometimes we just amuse ourselves; someone laughs, even if that someone is me." If I'd been there I would have fallen off the chair laughing, and June and I would have been thrown out of the Bible study on our derrières.

At a church conference in Florida, a cute little lady who claimed to be in her seventies came up to me and commented on my rather (okay, *very!*) short skirt and very high-heeled shoes. "I'm just like you," she said. "I have great legs." (That was a new one!) With that she pulled her dress up to her undies and did a pirouette. Sure enough, her legs were as shapely as any Radio City Music Hall Rockette.

"I've been covering up these legs with long, dreary—she named her church denomination, one known to have a lot to say about *adornment*—skirts all my life, but today I'm gonna go out and buy me a dress that will show off my best feature—my legs."

Another time a gray-haired woman, also claiming to be in her seventies, stood on one foot and then the other till I finished signing books. She then pulled me into a corner, and with a look on her face that suggested she might be going to ask my help in overthrowing the government, whispered, "You're a prankster; I can tell you're a prankster. I'm just like you; I'm a prankster too!" She winked a conspiratorial wink.

"I want to tell you what I pulled on my husband," she said. "You'll love it, and you can do it to your husband when you get home." By this time, she's giggling and blushing, and I'm wondering what in the world she's going to say.

"I came in from shopping the other day and my husband said, 'What did you buy?' I said, 'I bought a two-piece red outfit. You're gonna love it!' He said, 'Well, try it on; I want to see it.' She gave a wicked little snicker: "I can't believe I'm telling you this, but I went in the bedroom, took off all my clothes, and put on *red knee socks*. Then I went prancing out right in front of him. He almost had a heart attack!"

I'll admit I was shocked out of my mind; this woman had "pillar of the church" written all over her! "I strutted around all over the place," she said, "and he just loved it. He still has a good laugh every time he thinks about it." Then she took hold of my arm and whispered, "I'd never tell my church friends that, they'd die; but I can tell you 'cause you're a prankster. Go home and try it. Your husband will just love it."

I know what you're wondering, and my answer is, "None of your business."

It makes me sad to think there are women in their seventies who have spent a lifetime of energy holding back instead of letting go. And it's probably because years ago someone pronounced a

disapproving "Tsk, Tsk," and it became a curse on their lives.
Maybe it wasn't an audible click of the tongue, perhaps it was a
wag of the finger, or a disparaging "look" to put them in their
place—and they've been stuck in that "place" for fifty years. It
makes me so sad to think about this, that I'm crying as I write—
I was there!—I was a victim of the tsk-tsk-ers! And just when I
thought I had steeled myself against those who so destroyed my
spirit as a young woman—just when I thought I could laugh at
their "church-lady" self-righteous ways—I was slammed against
the wall and the old feelings came back.

I was attending my aunt's funeral, and afterward as lunch
was being served, a colorless (I'm not being catty; I'm just reporting!) little woman sat down beside me and began to chit-chat. It
soon became obvious that she thought I wasn't a Christian and
that I might be an easy evangelism target. *This was a funeral, for
heaven's sake, so what else could I be thinking but about my own soul and
where I would be spending eternity.* Just as she got to the get-your-
heart-right-with-God-or-else part, I decided it was time to cir-
cumvent—grab the ball and make an end run, so to speak.

"It's rather exciting," I said in my most sanctimonious tone
of voice, "to know my aunt is in heaven. How happy my parents
must be to see her, and how glorious the reunion with them and
the Lord." For a moment, I thought the woman had choked; she
took a huge gulp and made the most ghastly sound. I waited for
her to grab her throat signaling the international code for chok-
ing, but she seemed to be breathing. Maybe hyperventilating!
And waving her fork back and forth in the air like she was
directing choir practice. Just as I was ready to call for help she
came to her senses, drew in her breath, and gave me the most
incredulous look you can imagine. "Oh, *you're* a Christian?" she
said, putting her hand over her heart on her flat little chest. "You
certainly don't *look* like one."

This exchange was like a stab to my heart. For a moment I
felt like a reject once more. A reject from the family of God, and
I don't ever want to feel that way again.

Let's put up signs in our churches that say, "No tsk-tsk-ing!", "No finger wagging!", "No disparaging words!", "No 'looks' [you know the kind] allowed here!", "No squelching of personalities and/or ideas!", "No put-downs permitted on the premises!", and "Only encouraging words spoken here." For me, maybe a sign that says "Stick a sock in it!" would be good.

If I've ever squelched another person's spirit in any way, help me forgive those who have made me feel like I'm a reject from your family. Forgive me *for being catty and calling it "reporting." Give me kind words and nods of affirmation for others. Thank you for Deb and Lee and Tanya and Tina and my new "old friend," June. Let us share fun and joy and wackiness that's off the charts even when others don't get it! Amen.*

WITH FRIENDS LIKE THAT, WHO NEEDS ENEMIES?

Don't tolerate people who try to run your life, ordering you to bow and scrape, insisting that you join their obsession with angels and that you seek out visions. They're a lot of hot air, that's all they are. They're completely out of touch with the source of life, Christ, who puts us together in one piece, whose very breath and blood flow through us.

COLOSSIANS 2:18 (THE MESSAGE)

SINCE I'VE BECOME AN author, it seems as though there are a lot of people who want to run my life. As the verse says, they want me to embrace their agenda or their obsession, whatever it might be. At best they expect me to put my stamp of approval on their beliefs. Even my publisher wants to run my life! They say, "Do as many radio and TV interviews, speaking engagements, public appearances, book signings, and supermarket grand openings [joking!] as possible so you'll become known and people will buy the book."

I said, "I can't! I'm terrified!"

They said, "You can. You have to. Don't worry, we'll help you. We'll give you a publicist! The publicist will tell you what to do and how to do it."

Sure enough, the next thing I know I get a big fat packet in the mail from the publicist. The very first page tells me how to dress. Me! How to dress! It said, "Dress a cut above the way you usually dress." I'm quite certain I have impeccable taste, but when the church choir had a tacky party, within fifteen minutes of the announcement six people called to borrow my clothes. I kept this fact to myself, however, and headed out to buy a new suit, a taupe-colored suit, which I wore to my first speaking engagement. Afterward, my friends came rushing up.

"Great suit," they said. They looked me up and down and all around.

"Expensive suit!" They caressed the fabric.

"Soooo tasteful!" They shook their heads in agreement.

"It doesn't look like you!" They howled as though they'd told the funniest of jokes.

I went out and bought a purple satin suit, and they say it's gaudy! My friends aren't just *trying* to run my life, they *are* running my life.

One of my first radio interviews was with a psychiatrist, and her lead-in (a total surprise to me) was that I was there to talk about *making friends with my pain*. Gee, I didn't even know you were supposed to be friends with your pain, much less admit it on live radio. I don't know about you, but pain is no friend to me!

Another time I was on a panel with other breast cancer survivors discussing how we had handled our illness on a day-to-day basis. One of the panelists was one of those women we all love to hate; a little too perfect, if you know what I mean. Perfect hair, perfect makeup, perfect suit, perfect shoes, perfect everything. Especially perfect answers! The rest of us could've stayed home and scrubbed our toilets. Each time a question was asked, she would lean forward—as though she was going to swallow the microphone, for heaven's sake!—and say, "I can answer that." Then she would bat her eyelashes and smile a sappy smile, and give, what in my opinion was, a rather sappy answer. (I'm not being catty—I'm reporting!)

"Did you worry that you might die?" asked our hostess.

"I can answer that!" (*Lean forward, bat eyelashes, smile sappy smile.*) "No, I knew I wouldn't die! I had all my wonnnn-derful friends praying, and I knew I would be healed."

"Were you sick from chemotherapy?"

"I can answer that." (*Lean forward, bat eyelashes, smile sappy smile.*) "I was never sick a day. I had all my wonnnn-derful friends praying. No, never sick a minute!"

"Sue, how about you? Were you sick?"

"Weeell! Yes, I was! I had all my wonderful friends praying too, but boy was I ever sick! I'm talkin' sick! I threw up my toenails! I lived in front of the toilet! That thing was like some porcelain goddess demanding my worship—on my knees, twenty-four hours a day. I just hung over that commode night and day, turned green . . . thought my eyeballs would pop right out of the sockets. I was so sick . . ."

"Well, thank you, Sue, let's just move on. Ladies, how did your husbands respond to the fact you'd lost a breast?"

"I can answer that!" (*Lean forward* . . . you know the routine.) "My husband just adores me. Never loved me more. He said it was me he loved, not my breast, and that all he cared about was that I was alive and well."

"And Sue . . . ?"

"Well! My husband said, 'You lost a breast, you're outta here'!" *I'm joking!* I'm joking! Of course I didn't say that—neither did he! But you get the picture!

Sometimes I'm dealing with people who have their own "spiritual" agenda and want me to embrace it. Like the time I was doing a telephone interview with a radio station in Florida and the hostess's first words were, "Today we have with us author Sue Buchanan. Sue, after reading your book, *I'm Alive and the Doctor's Dead,* I can tell that you believe as we do, that it's not God's will for anyone to ever be sick or die." Eeeek! Is that what my book said? Maybe I should reread it! I gulped a few times and blubbered some inane thing; I have no idea what. It's not what I believe at all!

It's important to remember that God's agenda is the only right and perfect one and we can trust his plan completely. He guides us and gives us insight through his Word and through prayer and meditation. There will always be those who want to push their ideas in your face and expect you to embrace them, and some of them are right and good, but they should be examined carefully in light of God's Word and his plan for our lives. We must learn to recognize those who are "full of hot air!"

Dear Lord

In theory I know you are the only One qualified to judge, to say someone is "full of hot air." Only you are qualified to say who is "out of touch with the source of life." But you know me! I'm always eager to make those judgments without checking with you first! Your agenda is right and perfect. Help me recognize it; give me a good perspective on it, so that I'm "not out of touch, but focused on Christ, the source of life." Sometimes I have fun at another person's expense. (I've been known to do a pretty good imitation of "Miss Perfect" with her perfect answers), especially when I feel I'm being manipulated. Give me a gracious spirit. Amen.

A SHARP TONGUE KINDLES A GOOD NEWSPAPER COLUMN

A gentle response defuses anger, but a sharp tongue kindles a temper-fire.

PROVERBS 15:1 (THE MESSAGE)

IN NASHVILLE WE HAVE a free weekly newspaper called *The Scene.* To many, it's more important than the "real" newspaper. It not only lists practically every event that's ever being thought of in our town, but it has the best restaurant reviews and the most in-depth (if a tad left wing) investigative reporting.

One regular column (my favorite) is called "Ticked Off!" which allows you to call or write to "gripe, grouse, whine, belly-ache, criticize, condemn, dress down, or blow-up at anything you're ticked off at."

Each week I look forward to seeing what people are ticked off about. It can be a diatribe about the lottery—that it's the rich people who are voting it down because they don't want poor people to win, get rich, then move into *their* neighborhoods. Or it can be as simple as a gripe against women who wear sleeveless shirts and don't shave their armpits. That would tick off anyone.

Sometimes a battle goes on for weeks. One week there will be several Baptists angry that beer is being sold at the Arena—which is practically in the front yard of First Baptist Church—infringing on a law that prohibits selling beer within so many feet of a church.

The next week, the beer drinkers say that Baptists should be thanking them because (Duh!) it makes evangelism a cinch when the sinners are right there in their own front yard. That in turn brings about a rather un-Christian-like response from the other side, and back and forth it goes. Talk about a sharp tongue kindling a temper-fire!

Personally I can get quite upset about umbrellas. I think they should be public property. Say, let the government provide them (one apiece and a few extras) with the expectation that they be circulated. When you finish with one, wherever you are, you leave it by the door for the next person, or for the next time you need it.

I know! I know! There would then have to be policing and the next thing you know we'd all be communists! I just really get ticked off when I'm in the store and the umbrella is in the car, or when I have to go home to get the umbrella and it stops raining by the time I get there.

Bathroom fans tick me off too! They should all be disconnected, banned for false advertising. They don't do away with odors like they are supposed to, they only move them around. They're noisy to boot! And another thing I'm ticked about is Tupperware—mad that people are so selfish with it. Women go ballistic when they are missing one piece of Tupperware. They'll accuse you of stealing right to your face!

I'd never make accusations, but my pie keeper with the snap-on handle for easy transport walked away at the last Give Till It Hurts Lottie Moon supper and hasn't been seen since. Tupperware doesn't just walk away by itself, you know.

In my opinion, anything that is plastic and burps should be public property. Think of it! What a blessing it would be if everyone, when it came their way, would fill that Tupperware with something good and keep it circulating! The government wouldn't even have to provide it; there's already enough out there to go around many times over.

In almost every case, what people really need when they gripe, grouse, whine, bellyache, criticize, condemn, dress down, or blow-up is someone to care. Someone to say, "There, there!" They need a gentle response! And do you know what? Nothing ticks me off more than when someone doesn't give a gentle response. Har-umppph! WHAT'S WITH THESE PEOPLE? I MEAN IT'S NOT LIKE IT'S HARD OR ANYTHING! GOOD GRIEF! IT'S SIMPLE, ANYONE CAN DO IT. HOW STUPID CAN THEY BE? *DON'T THEY KNOW A SHARP TONGUE KINDLES A TEMPER-FIRE, FOR HEAVEN'S SAKE?*

Dear Lord

Being "ticked-off" isn't on your list of the fruit of the Spirit. I'm not telling you anything you don't know, but I often get worked up over the smallest of things and I gripe, grouse, bellyache, and on down the list. It's a very self-centered, time-consuming distraction from what I should be doing and thinking. Forgive me and change me. As for how I respond to others, Father God, take away the sharp retort that always seems to be on the tip of my tongue. Replace it with a "there, there"—a gentle response. Amen.

AFTER YOU'VE GONE THROUGH 6,000 BRILLO PADS, YOU AUTOMATICALLY QUALIFY FOR A PAIR OF STUART WEITZMAN SHOES

If someone has a hundred sheep and one of them wanders off, doesn't he leave the ninety-nine and go after the one? And if he finds it, doesn't he make far more over it than over the ninety-nine who stay put? Your Father in heaven feels the same way. He doesn't want to lose even one of these simple believers.

MATTHEW 18:12–14 (THE MESSAGE)

I CAN'T RELATE TO sheep, but if I had a hundred pair of shoes and lost one pair, I would go after a new pair! And if I found the lost shoes I would keep the replacement pair. I'm joking! Seriously, I really can relate to being the lost sheep! If you've ever been lost in a parking garage, I think you can safely say you know what it feels like to be lost!

Often when I'm in a distant city, I'll be driving along in my rental car and I'll spot a mall. Suddenly I'm possessed! New territory! I gotta shop! I know I'm late for a business meeting, but does that stop me? I don't think so. I can do this shopping thing in a hurry. I've had experience. In fact, I can spot a pair of Stuart Weitzmans from miles away, and I can have those shoes bought and on my Visa card before you can say, "How about a pair of rhinestone pantyhose to go with 'em?"

159

I don't like to brag, but I can buy shoes without even trying them on. If the shoe is fabulous, the size doesn't matter. I wear a size 6 shoe, but a 7 feels so good that I buy a 7 1/2! And as for the guilt trip for spending soooo much money, I feel I deserve it after all those years of housework without pay. Do you have any idea how many Brillo pads I've gone through?

The problem comes after I've made my purchases and head back out to find my car. I can say with pride that I always remember to take note of which door of what store I came in, so the problem is not getting back outside. It's remembering where I parked and what the car looks like.

It's not so bad when you are in your own city in your own car, but believe me, all rental cars look alike. I can never remember if I was driving a tan Taurus, a red Riviera, a puce Peugeot, or *a yellow submarine*, for that matter! There I am looking out over an ocean of cars of all colors and sizes, and all I can remember is I parked between a shiny little BMW ragtop and a beat-up old green van. For the life of me, I can't see either one! I must admit I'm panicked, if only for a moment.

The only thing I know for sure is that all Budget cars have license plates that include the letters BRC and that Hertz cars have license plates that include HTZ. You can run up and down the rows, find the license plates, try the key, and if luck is on your side, you'll figure it out.

I know what you're thinking! It's really silly to compare the biblical story of the lost sheep to being lost in the parking lot of a shopping mall with your arms full of bags. Maybe not. It seems like the Lord always uses something extremely—*I'm talkin' extremely*—basic to make his point.

It's so simple: He is our Shepherd, we are his sheep, and he doesn't think of us in bunches or herds or gaggles or flocks or swarms or prides (as in lions) or schools (as in fish), pods, coveys, packs, or droves. *Or even congregations, thank heavens!* He knows us as individuals and loves us so much he laid down his life: "I am the Good Shepherd. The good Shepherd lays down his life for the sheep."

Dear Lord

Thank you once more for reminding me that your truths are simple. Thank you for hearing my lost cry, for recognizing my voice, for finding me, and for bringing me to your fold! Thank you for keeping me safe there in your arms. Thank you! Amen.

I'VE ALREADY TOLD YOU MORE THAN I KNOW

When words are many, sin is not absent, but he who holds his tongue is wise.

PROVERBS 10:19

WHEN IT COMES TO words and jewelry my philosophy is (Can you guess?) *more is better.* My friends and I talk a lot. We talk so much that one of us is always asking, "Did I tell you that already?" Peggy says now that we're getting older it doesn't matter. She says, "Tell it again, we won't remember anyway!"

We even have well-worn phrases "in the can" ready to use when the occasion arises, and we use them over and over. No matter how many times we hear them they still crack us up. If someone mentions "small talk," one of us will say, "There's no talk too small for me." If Peggy is explaining something and someone asks a question, invariably she'll say, "I've already told you more than I know."

Peggy's husband, Bob, who has passed away, used to say that Peg took up knitting so she would have something to think about while she talked. My husband has a well-used quip on the subject as well. When my girlfriends and I go out to dinner or leave on a trip, his parting words are sure to be "Don't you want me to go along so there'll be someone to listen?"

Sometimes Wayne will say that a person has "mental constipation and verbal diarrhea." Sometimes we laugh, *depending on who he's talking about.*

If one of us should say the words "hold your tongue," invariably someone will actually grab their tongue and go into some wordy soliloquy. It's not a pretty sight!

In many ways, in our circle of friends, you don't have to hold your tongue. You can say pretty much whatever is on your mind (as long as it's not hurtful to another person), and you won't be judged. We can tell when someone is just spouting off ("Oh Sue! You know you don't believe that. Get a life!"), and when someone is really searching for answers. Even then, we won't make you feel put down. Usually your dilemma will evoke a lively discussion with strong opinions. Scripture might be examined; a concordance or two dragged out; perhaps we'll pray together. Eventually you'll come to the right conclusion on your own, and, having gone through the process, your faith is stronger.

Recently a woman told me that when she brought up something that the others in her group held a position on (not theology, but more of a behavioral issue) one of the men shut her down completely. "That's not what *we* believe!" (with an emphasis on the *we*). No questions asked! It seems to me that if your beliefs don't hold up under questioning, it's time to reexamine your beliefs!

There are times in our circle of friends when I do have to (figuratively) hold my tongue—not say everything that comes to mind. When someone confides in me, I don't dare break that trust. I have to be careful not to tell stories that aren't mine to tell, especially in writing a book. I've had to check with a lot of people. How disheartening it would be if one of my friends or acquaintances should write their own book and have someone say, "I already read that in Sue's book."

I, for one, want to be wise about holding my tongue when it comes to gossip, when it comes to squelching another person's search for answers, when someone confides in me. And sometimes I need to hold my tongue just because I talk too much!

I want you to help me know when to hold my tongue, but what I'm really concerned about is my friends. Help them hold their tongues as well. They could ruin me! Amen.

HE GAVE SOME TO BE SPAM EATERS AND OTHERS TO BE BALONEY EATERS

It was he who gave some to be apostles,
some to be prophets, some to be evangelists,
and some to be pastors and teachers, to pre-
pare God's people for works of service, so
that the body of Christ may be built up.

EPHESIANS 4:11–12

IT'S PRETTY FUNNY WHEN you look around and see some of the people God has picked to serve him. I don't want to mention names, but take a look at the speakers and musicians he's using! Some of these people are really weird. Sometimes it's the least likely person imaginable. Like me, for instance—spiritually challenged me! Gloria insists she caught me discussing Darwin with great authority until it dawned on me that Darwin wasn't a new cosmetic company. Not true!

Before I became a speaker, I thought that when these people weren't actually speaking or singing, they were sitting around all dressed up and in deep theological conversation eating peeled grapes. I found out otherwise.

Picture this: Gloria, Joy, Peggy, Tanya Goodman Sikes, and I have just finished an all-day Women of Faith Intensive Seminar.

We're back at the hotel, we've taken off our makeup, we're bare-foot, in our baggy nightgowns, and we're ready to dig into the huge goodie basket provided by our hosts.

The basket is ripped open (we're starved) and we're pushing and shoving and elbowing each other out of the way like junior high school boys who haven't seen food in years. There's a plump little ham, an assortment of gourmet cheeses, specialty crackers and cookies, cocoa mix, candy, and a beautiful array of fruit.

The conversation—remember, it takes place while we're stuffing our faces—goes something like this:

"Mmmm, good ham."

"Mmmm, yeah!"

"Know what I like better 'n ham?"

"No, what?"

"Big ol' hunk-a baloney."

"I like Spam. D'ya'll like Spam? Spam on white bread!"

" . . . nothin' better."

" . . . all we could afford when we got married . . . got used to it . . . still like it."

"Mmmm, us too!"

"I make a good Spam casserole. Want my recipe? Spinach and Spam. Real good."

"D'ja-ever fry baloney?" There is a huge response to this; everyone has!

"Yeah, I like it when it curls up."

"Mmmm! Me too. I fill the cavity with Velveeta."

"That's my favorite. Didja know you can do it in the microwave? It'll curl just like it does in the skillet. That way you don't have to get the skillet dirty."

You get the picture! This Spam-baloney dialogue went on for forty minutes! Seriously! Forty minutes! So much for deep theological discussions and peeled grapes!

I often talk to people who tell me they are ordinary, that they have nothing to offer and couldn't possibly be used by God. The Gaithers were school teachers in Indiana. That's pretty ordinary!

Gloria thought she was a failure because she didn't get to realize her dreams either to go to the mission field or become a second Barbara Walters. Quite a gap there, Gloria! Yet God used her in a totally unexpected way as a lyricist, author, speaker, and as co-host of the Homecoming videos.

No one is ordinary in God's sight! It strikes me that God can use plain ol' simple Spam and baloney eaters as his servants every bit as well as he can use big ol' brainy theologians with their discussions about Darwin and their peeled grapes.

Dear Lord

I'm amazed at the people you choose to help build up the body of Christ. A pretty weird bunch! I'm in awe of the fact that I'm one of them. Thank you. Amen.

MY ROD AND MY REEL, THEY COMFORT ME

He said, "Throw your net on the right side
of the boat and you will find some [fish]."
When they did, they were unable to haul the
net in because of the large number of fish.

JOHN 21:6

I LOVE TO FISH! When I was three or four years old my grandpa used to put a safety pin on a string, tie it to a stick, sit me on a rock by the goldfish pond, and let me fish to my heart's content. I'm sure Grandpa knew I wouldn't be landing any of his prized goldfish with my safety pin, but later he took me to the creek and we caught fish like crazy. It instilled in me a love for fishing that has lasted a lifetime.

A couple of times I've had business trips to Florida and have added a fishing day. Once my daughter Dana and I spent a week in the Gulf Shores area fishing away our mornings out on one of those long concrete piers, and shopping away our afternoons in the boutiques and T-shirt stores.

Sometimes Wayne and I fish with our neighbors, Joe and Alice, and sometimes with our Chicago friend Dan, on his boat on Lake Michigan. Wherever, whenever; I love it. And it gives me a nice warm feeling to know Jesus and his cohorts were fishermen. I suppose they didn't really have a choice in the matter; if they didn't fish they didn't eat, whereas we have Mrs. Paul's.

When we take someone fishing for the first time we play a little trick on them by distracting them, tying a boot to the line, and then watching as they struggle to land the "the big one." Maybe Jesus and his buddies did the same thing with a sandal.

Sometimes I think they fished in their underwear—you know, boys will be boys!—because it says in John 21:7 that when Peter realized it was Jesus who was speaking to them, "he wrapped his outer garment around him (for he had taken it off) ..." Nevertheless I picture them having a good time.

On this particular day, when the nets were so full they couldn't haul them in, I can just see it! They were probably jumping all over that boat with excitement—like we do when someone yells "fish on," and we all get in each other's way trying to get to the same down-rigger—slipping this way and sliding that, and trying to hang on to that heavy net! It's a wonder the boat didn't capsize.

And I can just see them when they got to dry land, fish goo from head to toe, running around in circles trying to out-shout each other! They had the grand-daddy of all grand-daddies fish story and they had proof! They had witnessed a miracle. And to think they were telling the truth—which is something no other fisherman has done since!

A fisherman will say he had a "big catch" when he didn't catch a flea; that he "limited out," when he didn't come close. He'll tell you he caught a fish that weighed twenty-five pounds and was three feet long, when it was barely the size of a minnow. When you ask to see it, he'll brag that he "threw it back for the sake of ecology." And these are *Christian* fisherman I'm talking about here!

What happened in John 21:6 (and I only swallow it hook, line, and sinker because it's in the Bible) is probably the only honest-to-goodness, true fish story in the history of man, and it wasn't even really about fish. It was about a miracle! It was about Jesus taking some simple, ordinary, everyday thing and some very discouraged guys and working a miracle! He did it so that they would believe and spread the Word. "These are written that you may believe that Jesus is the Christ, the Son of God, and that by believing you may have life in his name" (John 20:31). Who better than fishermen to spread the Word?

Dear Lord

Thank you, O God, for the truth of your Son, that by believing we may have life in his name. You are an awesome God! Amen.

I COULD LOSE MYSELF IN THOUGHT, BUT THEN AGAIN, IT'S SUCH UNFAMILIAR TERRITORY

Therefore do not worry about tomorrow.
Each day has enough trouble of its own.

MATTHEW 6:34

WE HAVE ENOUGH TROUBLE goin' on today without worrying about tomorrow. My mother once said that she had been a worrier all her life, but that not one single thing she'd worried about had come true. She suggested that a lot of times worry is really an outgrowth of boredom. In her wise way, she suggested that keeping your mind busy and productive was a good antidote to worry, that "an idle mind is the devil's workshop."

It's true for me. I can go a little crazy, obsessing about the most insignificant things. Knowing my own weakness, however, I've developed a few little tricks to keep myself on track, telling myself there really is no excuse for being bored. I say that even if you are broke and have no friends, you can "people watch," and it can keep you busy for days on end. When I'm stuck in an airport for hours, and I've read all the magazines except *Popular Mechanics* and stuffed myself full of junk food, I like to find a seat in a high-traffic corridor and "people watch." I conjecture about their lives.

Oh, she isn't really a nun. She's with the FBI. That rosary in her hand is a two-way radio, and under that habit, there's enough ammunition to take down half of Central America. Then I try to figure out who the others are in the waiting area and which ones are part of her cartel. It's gotta be a big operation, otherwise how did she get security clearance?

I like to try to guess what people are thinking, too. Sometimes I carry it a step further. I eavesdrop. I stand in a telephone booth with a phone to my ear pretending to make a call and listen to the people on either side of me.

It can be pretty disconcerting to hear the person on one side of you screaming, "Pick it up, woman! I know you're there. Wait till I get my hands on you!" while on the other side a man is telling his wife (or girlfriend?) what she should be wearing when he arrives home—and it's not flannel jammies he's describing either!

My favorite is the big business mugga-mugga, with the Gucci briefcase, who talks to his child like he's an idiot. "Gagagagaga. Dada on twippy. Big pwane. Dada wuv u too. Dada wuv Mama. Dada tumming home—big, big pwane." That's when you lean forward and say, "Excuse me, do you have change for a dollar?" They'll swallow the phone every time.

If you get bored at a ball game, you can stand outside the men's room and count how many men check their zippers as they come out the door. You'll be surprised; almost all do.

When I see people just staring into space, I wonder what they are thinking. Sometimes I just have to ask them. I was with friends at a flea market in Texas and got bored with shopping. I told them I'd meet them later—that I was going to write a book on what men think about while their wives shop, and I needed to do research. They bought it, and I struck out on my own.

All the men I talked to were more than willing to cooperate. Of course, I told them I was writing a book! I got short answers: "I think I'm fixin' to go crazy." And I got long answers: "Well, I'm a deer hunter. I'm thinkin' 'bout when I go deer huntin'— makin' a mental list of supplies 'n stuff. Yer five *hunert* miles from home and ya gotta take food 'n ever'thing." He began to list "everything" and my eyes glazed over—bedding, salt, flour, catsup, containers, soap, bug spray, pills if you get sick, etc. "Yer sixtysome miles from the near'st phone so ya cain't fergit nothin'. 'Course, ya gotta take yer gun 'n yer *amanition*" . . . and on and on.

Some of the men I talked to felt it was a give-and-take situation: "I can't complain 'cause she went to the drag races with me last night." Or, "She said she'd make it up to me tonight." (Blush!) "What I mean is she's gonna fix me a big ol' chicken dinner."

"C'mere and sit down," said one old-timer. "See that step over there? I've been sittin' here since noon. Watch. Every third person trips on it." Sure enough!

There were philosophical answers: "I'm sittin' here thinkin' women are real intelligent. You have to watch 'em to figure that out. Sometimes you just need to be quiet and watch to appreciate them." Another philosopher said, "I watch everybody and try to figure out their feelings. People can be real funny looking, but everybody has feelings—regardless."

I decided to stop my research when a big old country boy pulled me down beside him, took my hand in his and whispered in my ear: "I was just sitting here wishing a good lookin' blonde-haired woman would come by and tell me she was writing a book and ask me what I was thinking."

Perhaps we should concentrate on stuffing our minds with good books and good conversation so there is no space for worries. Maybe we could sing praise songs and hymns as we go about our mindless tasks, and when worries sneak in through the cracks, perhaps we could utter this prayer:

Dear Lord

I'm worrying again. Not just about today, but about tomorrow and about every day for the next ten years! What will happen here? What will happen there? Take my worry thoughts and turn them to praise thoughts to you. You know the future and you have everything under control. Amen.

AS NOAH SAID TO HIS WIFE, "WOODPECKERS COULD ACTUALLY BE A BIGGER THREAT THAN THE STORM ITSELF!"

The Lord then said to Noah, "Go into the ark, you and your whole family, because I have found you righteous in this generation."

GENESIS 7:1

THE PASSAGE IN GENESIS where God gives Noah all the instructions about building the ark is very interesting, considering the fact there had never been a flood before. He tells him how long, how wide, and how high it should be, what to make it out of, how many decks it should have, and how it should be finished off. He tells him to get on the boat with his family and two of every animal (seven of some) and enough food to last more than forty days.

At first it sounds cozy, like the cruise you always hoped to take. Perhaps the first couple of days it was, but for whatever it's worth, my guess is that the trip went downhill really fast from there. I think there was a lot left out of the story in the retelling. I don't mean that Noah wasn't righteous, but he wasn't perfect. I don't mean that it didn't happen the way

Scripture says it happened. I'm just saying there were bound to be a few details missing in the retelling!

Noah was six hundred years old, so probably when he suggested building this boat he was questioned a lot.

"Excuse me?" I can hear Shem say. "Dad, are you sure you heard right? You know how bad your hearing is."

"We're doin' whut?" Noah's wife, who had probably gotten comfortable in retirement, pipes in. "He's deaf all right. I call it 'selective hearing' because, like most old men, he only hears what he wants to."

Shem's wife adds her two cents: "No, he's senile; that's what. He is senile!"

Then there was the (excuse the expression) poop. There had to have been a lot of discussion about that, considering all the animals.

"My wife says we'd better have a plan for that or she stays home," Ham snarls. "She says it's either her or the elephants."

"Well, we know they can't hang over the side, so somebody better make a plan," reasons Japheth. "I'm busy with the grocery order."

Somehow it gives me a good feeling to create these little scenarios that let me think of these people as human and yet know they were righteous people that God used in a remarkable way. When I think of the Old Testament characters—and let's face it, many of them *were* characters—it makes me think that if God could use them, he could use a character like me.

Dear Lord

It says that Noah was a righteous man, blameless among the people of his time, and he walked with God. I want to walk with you. I want to be your person. Amen.

WANTED: OFFICIAL CHURCH QUIPSTER; NO EXPERIENCE NEEDED

The light shines in the darkness, but the darkness has not understood it.

JOHN 1:5

THERE ARE CHURCHES ALL over Nashville with neon-lit signs (often they're on poles way up in the air). They say the most ridiculous things. Who writes these inane sayings? The minister? Is there a course in seminary that teaches how to write these quips? Introduction to Quip Outreach? Advanced Quip Outreach? Are there official church quipsters? Perhaps there are laypersons who have gone to the altar to dedicate their lives to coming up with these things?

One sign near my house reads, "We aren't Dairy Queen, but we have good SUNDAYS." Another says, "Turn right and go straight." You could wreck your car if you aren't careful! My question is, "Are we speaking of your car or your life?" The way the sign is placed, if you turn right and continue straight it will take you into the church parking lot. Maybe they think if they get you into the parking lot, they can get you into church.

On the other hand, "Turn right and go straight" could be an admonishment to do what's right, as opposed to what's wrong, and walk the straight and narrow. In that case, of course, you would end up in church, so they have you one way or another. Somehow, I doubt the quipster realized the cleverness of the double meaning. *"Oh, yeah! That too, duh! Didn't think of that."*

Less than a mile away another sign reads: "Doest what thou shalt doeth, as thou doest it, for his name's sake." Last month it said: "For unto the lilies God gaveth as unto the hills." What kind of double talk is that? It's certainly flowery, and you'll have to admit it sounds spiritual, but duh! What does it mean? I could surely *doeth* better than that if I were the quipster!

Next door to that one is a similar sign that says "Get relief from back pain." No wait! That's the sign for the chiropractor. Well, duh number two! At least you can understand *it*.

My favorites are the ones with misspelled words: "Potluck supper at six: prayer and medication to follow" or "To those who enjoy sinning—please come for choir practice."

Then there's WWJD? Even though I now know what it means, for a long time I thought it was an advertisement for a radio station. Sometimes it's spelled out: "What Would Jesus Do?" My reaction to that is (and I've been known to talk back to these signs), "I think I pretty much know what he would do. I just don't always do it."

We aren't always "user friendly" when it comes to reaching out to our nonbelieving friends. It must be very confusing to them when they read our signs and listen to our clichés; they must think we speak some secret language. Perhaps we do. It's no wonder the light shines in darkness but the darkness hasn't understood it. We've simply made it too confusing. Or stupid maybe! Getteth thou my drift?

Aesthetically the signs don't work for me, but if—I'm saying if—they have to be there why not settle for Scripture? Some churches do. Yesterday I saw a sign that said: "Come unto me,

all you who are weary and burdened and I will give you rest"
(Matthew 11:28). You'll have to agree that's pretty appealing! We
all live life in the fast lane these days; we're weary and burdened
and most people don't have a clue where to find rest from the rat
race. Maybe I'm wrong, but I don't think they'll get it from a
verse on a signpost!

But duh number three! What if they read the sign and make
the connection to me? To you? To those of us who know him?
They see that the verse is true because of the way we live. They
see that we have found rest and contentment in the Lord.
Because of our example, they'll want to *turn right and go straight!*
They may even want to go to church!

Dear Lord

*Help us to examine the way we do things. You must laugh.
Sadly, so does the unbeliever. I want to be one of your exam-
ples, someone whose faith speaks and, through my witness, who
is appealing to others. Let me be light in a dark world. Amen.*

PRESS TWO TO TRY OUT FOR THE EASTER PAGEANT

*Paul, Silas and Timothy, To the church of
the Thessalonians in God the Father and
the Lord Jesus Christ: ... We always thank
God for all of you, mentioning you in our
prayers.*

1 THESSALONIANS 1:1–2

IT'S FUN TO READ other people's mail, and while 1 Thessalonians isn't exactly a personal letter (it's to the whole Thessalonian church), it's interesting; and surprisingly, it's as relevant today as it was then. Well, maybe not *surprisingly*—it's God's Word, for heaven's sake!

For instance, in chapter five of 1 Thessalonians, it says to "... be joyful always; pray continually; give thanks in all circumstances, for this is God's will for you in Christ Jesus." Well, duh! It could have been written yesterday.

This letter was written long before Fed Ex, Priority, snail mail (U.S. postal), or even Pony Express, so it's hard to tell how long it took to get to its destination—and surprising that it got there at all. Another thought: Were there envelopes? I don't think so. It must have traveled from hand to hand, donkey to donkey, caravan to caravan. Wait! Now that I think about it, maybe it got there quicker than it would today.

Today Paul (who wrote this letter) wouldn't even write, he'd call. He would simply pick up the phone and beep one of the elders, or leave a message on the church answering machine.

"Hello. You've reached the Church of Thessalonica. We're not here at the moment. Press one for a list of activities. Press two if you want to try out for the Easter pageant. Press three to sign up for the Wednesday night class: 'Put Paganism in the Past.' Press four to leave a message."

Well, it's a thought! I, for one, am glad for the letters and that they are part of God's plan for revealing himself, which is what the Bible is all about.

Thank you that your Word is as relevant today as it was back then. That you are as relevant! This is no coincidence. It's part of this wonderful plan of yours. Thank you, O God! Amen.

PETITE PAW PRINTS IN THE PERFECT PUMPKIN PIE

In my Father's house are many rooms; if it
were not so, I would have told you. I am
going there to prepare a place for you.

JOHN 14:2

CHRISTMAS AT OUR HOUSE is the highlight of the year. Dana and Barry come from out of town, and in-town family members pack their suitcases and "move in" too. This includes Mindy, my brother, Jon, my sister-in-law, Becky, and my teenage nieces, Cara and Kirby, who are the joy of my life. Everybody stays for several days—sometimes until New Year's.

Wayne and I work hard ahead of time to get things ready. We decorate the house inside and out; he puts garlands on the stairway, I decorate the tree and, as he puts it, "every flat surface in the house." Actually it's not just flat surfaces I decorate; I hang stuff in windows, on doorknobs, and from chandeliers. (I have a friend who has special holiday seat covers for her bathrooms but I haven't gotten that carried away yet!) Wayne drapes the shrubbery with little white lights, the front door with garlands, and sets the big red-nosed Rudolph at the edge of the hill where it can be seen long before you turn into the driveway.

We grocery shop till the pantry and all the cabinets are full and the refrigerator is overflowing. We even stash supplies in big baskets in the kitchen corners and in the hall closet. We make candy and cookies, cranberry relish and homemade noodles. We boil the sweet potatoes, tear up the bread for dressing, make lists, and wrap packages. We even put bows on the cats' collars!

Jon and Becky make preparations, too. They fix their specialties: zucchini bread, corn pudding, cheese grits for breakfast, and— our favorite—Mama's pumpkin pies. Mother was famous for her pies, and although she's in heaven now, we've vowed to keep the art of pie-making alive and pass it on to future generations. If I remember correctly Mother used canned pumpkin, but the Davises, being "pumpkin snobs," buy a pumpkin and cook it themselves!

At our house, *the more people the merrier,* and in years past, Becky's dad and stepmother, CB and Anita, joined us.

The first Christmas they spent with us, their little Taco Bell dog, Teeny, was a member of their family, which presented a bit of a problem. As Christmas drew near and as plans were being made, it became clear that Teeny was not going to be put in a kennel, as Jon had strongly suggested. (In your mind's eye please think of Hitler *strongly suggesting* and you'll have a clear picture of Jon!) Teeny would be coming regardless of how the family felt, and the family (cat lovers, all) had had experience with Teeny before, and henceforth had described her as "that nervous little rat of a dog that barks all the time." Now that I think of it, that's probably one of the nicer things that was said!

CB, Anita, and Teeny came early and spent a couple of days at Jon and Becky's before moving to our house on Christmas Eve. During that time, it became great entertainment for Wayne and me to get frequent phone calls from Jon reporting on "that dog"! Let me explain that by now Jon, who doesn't have a mean bone in his body, had developed something of a comedy routine with Teeny as the ... what? The fall guy? Fall dog? Scapegoat?

Scapedog? I don't know, but I can tell you Jon is very funny—he could be a stand-up comedian—and he was playing this one to the hilt.

The last report we had gotten, before we saw them coming up the driveway—three vehicles laden with food and gifts and people—was that "that dog" would not be making the final trek to our house. There wasn't a dog living that would get the better of Jon! No siree! He would be the victor! Teeny would be locked in the bathroom alone with a little food and a lot of newspapers. In my brother's words: "It's time she finds out the truth about Santa Claus and learns to deal with it!"

When Jon walked in he was carrying two foil-covered pumpkin pies and he was livid. He was ranting and raving (fortunately out of earshot of his in-laws), and *fit to be tied*. "That dog" had jumped over the seat into the back of the station wagon and walked all over the pies. "Ruined!" he said. "The pies are ruined! Throw them in the garbage!"

Thankfully, I managed to rescue the pies just before they landed in the trash and Dana distracted Jon by stuffing his mouth with cheese puffs and smoked salmon hors d'oeuvres. Although the aluminum foil was caved in a couple of places, as far as I could see, not an iota of damage had been done to the pies.

Much to our surprise Teeny behaved like a trooper, and although I can't say our two cats were hospitable (they pretty much stayed out of sight), there was no hissing or scratching. The next day we stuffed ourselves with Christmas dinner, and then it was time for pie and coffee. And time to play a trick on Jon! He fell right into our hands when he offered to help serve dessert. Dana was ready for him! When he walked into the kitchen she handed him a pie server, a bowl of whipped cream, and a pie, which she presented with something of a flourish. She had taken three fingers and made little doggie paw tracks all the way across the top.

Jon didn't disappoint us! He came unglued—went berserk! At least as berserk as you can go with your in-laws sitting patiently in the next room waiting for their pie.

Christmas at our house is just a tiny little hint of what God is preparing for us in heaven. The planning will be impeccable. The cabinets, the pantry, the refrigerator, the baskets in the corner, and the closet in the hall will be full to overflowing, and think of the fun we'll have! Eternal celebration and joy! And the pie? Surely there will be pie in heaven, or at least the *heavenly equivalent* of pie (Who knows, maybe Mama's pie?). This I know: it will be perfect!

I can't begin to understand the preparation that's being made for me in heaven. I can only compare it to the things I know here on earth, and perhaps Christmas is a glimpse of what is to come. Let me be prepared and let me show others the way. When it comes to heaven, the more the merrier! *Amen.*

TO PLAY EVE IN THE CHURCH MUSICAL, IT WILL BE NECESSARY TO HAVE LONG HAIR

So God created man in his own image, in the image of God he created him; male and female he created them.

GENESIS 1:27

SEVERAL TIMES IN MY life, I've been an atheist—maybe for only five minutes, but nevertheless for that moment, I didn't believe in God. I thought, "Wow, this redemption story sounds just too good to be true; I just can't believe it." A few times I was an atheist because things all around me were going dreadfully wrong. I thought, "There is no God; if there were, none of this would be happening."

When I seriously doubt the existence of God, all I have to do is "people watch." *Yep, there's a God all right; who else would have thought of that exact combination of body parts—put together in that exact way?*

Wonder what Adam and Eve looked like? They must have been perfect. I'm sure in today's world, they would easily make *People* magazine's fifty most beautiful people. I've seen pictures of Eve in Bible story books. In some, she's a blonde; in others she's a brunette. Whatever the color, her hair is always long and fluffy so it will hang down over the front of her and cover her breasts for the sake of modesty. For awhile there she was naked, you know.

This doesn't have anything to do with anything—a side bar, so to speak—but Eve was the only woman without a past (just an interesting thing to think about). She could never throw it up to Adam how good she had it at home. I do think the Adam-and-Eve account is another case where we've been given "just the facts, ma'am," and that the Bible doesn't tell us everything. Like how long it took Eve to get over her pout after her whiny husband blamed her (and it was God to whom he was ratting, for heaven's sake) for the garden incident. Maybe she was more forgiving than I would be. They had a baby not too long after, so that should tell us something. Wonder who got blamed for that?

I've heard the only reason God gave Adam a wife was that he knew if the world was to be populated, he would have to invent a woman. Men wouldn't have the stamina to go through pregnancy and childbirth. Another little side bar for whatever it's worth: Eve was probably the first woman with stretch marks! At that point she probably thanked her lucky stars she wasn't still running around naked. Another reason to give Adam a wife (and on a more mundane level), as keeper of the grounds, Adam would need someone to help him remember where he put the garden tools. Or someone to blame if he couldn't *find* the tools!

Dear Lord

It seems as though Adam and Eve enjoyed walking with you as long as you were going their direction, instead of the other way around. I find myself in the same exact situation. Help me walk with you regardless. Amen.

AND AFTER THIS WILL COME MY SIX-VOLUME BIBLE COMMENTARY

The Lord bless you and keep you; the Lord make his face shine upon you and be gracious to you; the Lord turn his face toward you and give you peace.

NUMBERS 6:24–26

IT'S BEEN FIVE MONTHS since I signed a contract to deliver this book. That's fast, but as I explained to my editor, I have a short attention span, so it's now or never.

I'm often asked, "How do you write a book?" The only answer I can give is, "Keep your derrière on the chair." That and Snickers bars in the freezer.

My husband has been great. His health has improved. What I thought was a terminal case of *whileyerup* disease is almost gone. You know: "Whileyerup get me a glass of water"; "Whileyerup turn the air conditioning down." His mustard-Alzheimer's has gotten better too. That's the malady that causes him to stand in front of the refrigerator and yell, "Where's the mustard?"

He has grocery shopped, cooked, and done laundry; perhaps if I write another book, he'll learn to fold. He still chews me out for the missing socks, but I keep my mouth shut and smile sweetly. I know not to go there. Duh! *Fools rush in where fools belong,* is my motto.

When the manuscript was finished, he spell-checked, formatted, and fixed my punctuation, taking out over a hundred exclamation marks! In fact, I gave him a whole page of commas, periods, colons, semicolons, question marks, and exclamations, and said, "Put them wherever you jolly well please."

I've had a blast writing this book, but there is something I must tell you. I've spent the better part of a lifetime playing the role of an intellectually-challenged dumb blonde, not only in everyday actions, but spiritually as well. I didn't have a clue as to what God's will was for my life. In fact, I spent years being careful *not to find out* what God had in mind for me. Eeeek! He might ask me to be a missionary in some pagan land (A pagan land to me is a place without beauty shops!), or he might ask me to give up my big earrings, or my leopard skin underwear. Heaven forbid!

Sixteen years ago, I had cancer, and the experience changed my life—my heart. I began to ask questions and—Surprise! Surprise!—I've been *thinking* occasionally! I feel as if I've been spiritually asleep from birth and have been waking up in increasingly larger increments; awake longer each time.

In *An American Childhood,* Annie Dillard writes:

> Children ten years old wake up and find themselves here, discover themselves to have been here all along; is this sad? They wake like sleepwalkers, in full stride; they wake like people brought back from cardiac arrest or from drowning: *in media res,* surrounded by familiar people and objects, equipped with a hundred skills. They know the neighborhood, they can read and write English, they are old hands at the commonplace mysteries, and yet they feel themselves to have just stepped off the boat, just converged with their bodies, just flown down from a trance, to lodge in an eerily familiar life already well under way.

I woke in bits, like all children, piecemeal over the years. I discovered myself and the world, and forgot them, and discovered them again. I woke at intervals until, by that September when Father went down the river, the intervals of waking tipped the scales, and I was more often awake than not. I noticed this process of waking, and predicted with terrifying logic that one of these years not far away I would be awake continuously and never slip back, and never be free of myself again.

So maybe I *am* just coming alive—just now waking up spiritually—and what I'm finding out is not terrifying. It's so simple! So simple a shallow person can understand it. What I've found out about God is that he is totally trustworthy, and I can relax in his plans. And besides that, all he wants is—are you ready for this?—for me to be his person. *Just be his person, for heaven's sake!* Furthermore, I don't have to be brilliant or have a theology degree; he's given me this wonderful guidebook, his Holy Word!

All I can say to that is, Duh! Who knows? Next I may be writing a six-volume Bible commentary!

For those who read this book I pray:

"The Lord bless you and keep you; the Lord make his face shine upon you and be gracious to you; the Lord turn his face toward you and give you peace" (Numbers 6:24–26). Amen.

Friends Through Thick and Thin

by Gloria Gaither, Peggy Benson,
Sue Buchanan, and Joy MacKenzie

"The four of us are as different as spring, summer, winter, and fall, but we are the best of friends. Joy is the most organized, Peggy is our storyteller historian, Gloria is by far the most intellectual. As for me, I may as well tell you, I'm shallow!"
—Sue

The authors, who have been good friends for over thirty years, celebrate the ups and downs and all-arounds of friendship: how they've cheered each other on in good times, supported each other in hard times, and shared heartaches, fun, and laughter through it all.

This book spotlights the friendships that add beauty, meaning, and sanity to our daily lives. The four women are all mothers of grown children, authors, public speakers, avid readers, and lovers of music, discount shopping, and long days at the seashore. With warmth, humor, and wisdom they share the secrets they've learned about lasting friendship over the years.

Friends Through Thick and Thin is an encouraging look at one of life's greatest gifts: friendship. Sit back and revel in this joyous, personal time of sharing with four extraordinary women.

Hardcover 0-310-21726-1
Softcover 0-310-22865-4

I'm Alive and the Doctor's Dead

by Sue Buchanan

This book is here to say, Ignore the nay-sayers, ignore the statistics. The computer doesn't know you. . . . Cherish the moments and look for the rainbows.
As for statistics, it's all just fairy dust. —From the book

When the doctor pronounces a patient "as good as dead," does she have to take it lying down? "No way!" says Sue Buchanan, who outlived the doctor who predicted she'd die of breast cancer more than fifteen years ago.

I'm Alive and the Doctor's Dead is a high-spirited manifesto for any woman facing a medical verdict she doesn't want to hear. Buchanan tells her story

and assures women that there is life—and a lot of it—during and after cancer. Warm, funny, and very, very honest, this encouraging book offers practical help and hope for women suffering from breast cancer.

"Sue put me smack in the middle of every situation: the denial, the doctor's offices, the funny shenanigans, the best friends . . . Every person, male or female, should read this enlightening, encouraging, and hilarious book."
—Thelma Wells, Author and Speaker

"This book is rich in a commodity often in short supply for those facing cancer: HOPE."
—Dave Dravecky, Author, Founder of Outreach of Hope

"Sue's account of her courageous, head-on battle against cancer should benefit and inspire thousands.   "
—Jerry B. Jenkins, Author, Left Behind Series

Softcover 0-310-22455-1

Girls Gotta Have Fun!
101 Great Ideas for Celebrating Life with Your Friends

by Sue Buchanan

Coming Soon! January 2000

Sue Buchanan is absolutely the world's authority on the subject of friendship. Why? Because she has absolutely the world's best friends! She and her gal pals are always thinking up ways to stay connected—silly ways, serious ways, spiritual ways, cheap ways, and even a few expensive ways. *Girls Gotta Have Fun!* bubbles over with ideas for celebrating joys with friends.

As a speaker, Sue is invariably asked the same question: "How can I create the kind of rich, fun friendships you talk about?" Women, Sue has discovered, are hungry to know more about the art of friendship. Some of her ideas are pure fun, like leaving a message on a friend's answering machine using a foreign accent. Others are more serious, like writing out a prayer for a chum in need.

This book is ready to help instill encouragement and fun in a friendship, strengthening the wonderful, magical bond that exists between girls of all ages.

Hardcover 0-310-22895-9

We want to hear from you. Please send your comments about this book to us in care of the address below. Thank you.

ZondervanPublishingHouse
Grand Rapids, Michigan 49530
http://www.zondervan.com